P9-CMB-407

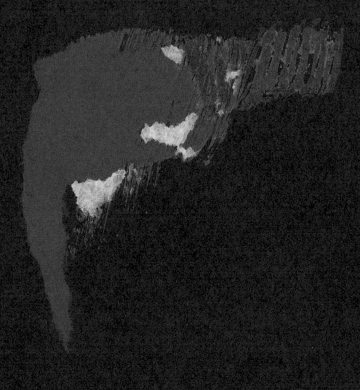

A GUIDE TO THE FINANCIAL MARKETS

Charles R. Geisst

St. Martin's Press   New York

Library of Congress Cataloging in Publication Data

Geisst, Charles R.
  Guide to the financial markets.

  Bibliography: p.
  Includes index.
  1. Capital market. 2. Hedging (Finance). I. Title.
II. Title: Financial markets.
HG4523.G44 1982   332.6'78   81−18514
ISBN 0−312−35294−8   AACR2

For the two Margarets

List of Figures

List of Tables

List of Tables

Contents

Acknowledgements

A book of so diverse a nature as this owes a debt of gratitude to many people, too numerous to mention. However, special thanks are in order to Michael Schwartz of L. F. Rothschild, Unterberg, Towbin (New York); Brad Georges of ContiCommodity Services (London); William F. Kennedy of the University of North Carolina, Charlotte; and Geoff Henney of Chemical Bank Foreign Exchange Advisory Service (London), all of whom commented upon chapters concerned with their various specialities. I must emphasise that all comments, conclusions, and opinions voiced are solely my own and do not reflect those of the readers or of any institution. A special note of thanks is also in order to Rosemary Haynes, who painstakingly helped prepare the manuscript.

C. R. G.

Introduction

An understanding of the roles and functions of financial markets remains an elusive goal in so far as general public knowledge is concerned. Unlike politics and social trends, developments and even fundamentals of the markets tend to pass unnoticed by the public and remain topical only to those involved in the various aspects of the profession itself. When the activities of the markets and their effects do become topics for more generalised discussion, they are often relegated to a second place, cloaked behind more broadly based issues such as unemployment or the level of house mortgage rates; topics, which if not in themselves comprehensible to all, are at least more recognisable.

Despite this condition, no other area of endeavour other than politics directly or indirectly affects the lives of so many people. Aristotle's ageless dictum that man is a political animal could easily be rephrased to state that man is equally a financial animal because, as with politics, everything that he does in the contemporary world is affected by these international activities. But, unlike other organised disciplines of study, no one single frame of reference describes the financial markets as an activity unto themselves, worthy of study for that reason alone.

The causes of this neglect are not of immediate interest here; our interest lies in a methodology designed to cope with the problem, even if only in an imperfect manner. But perhaps one reason for this neglect should be mentioned because it indirectly becomes the format of this book. This has to do with how a financial market is defined. Suffice it to say that a financial market is an arena where financial instruments change hands. However, most studies attempting to tackle the subtleties of the markets have confined themselves to the *capital* markets; those arenas where money is raised for a company or government, whether it be equity or debt capital. These markets, namely the stock, money and bond markets, have been well examined in recent years although it must be said that most of the work falls into one of two camps. The first are

1

advanced studies, of little use to the introductory reader, while the second, more appropriate as introductions, are normally 'do-it-yourself' books designed to tell one all that is needed to make a quick fortune.

Three additional markets are discussed here; the commodity, foreign exchange and options markets, which are not capital markets since they do not raise new money, but are instead referred to as *hedging* markets, where holders of capital assets may mitigate the risk attached to holding them. Obviously, for this reason they are not involved in studies concerning capital markets but they cannot be ignored simply because they are not part of the capital raising process.

In the broadest sense, economic activity is dependent upon raising new money but cannot be fully understood or appreciated without a comprehension of the hedging markets. In the following chapters what has become known as the equity capital shortage, particularly in the United States, will be referred to several times. This means that equity financing as a part of a company's total capital structure has been falling off in recent years in favour of debt financing. Part of this problem is due to different tax treatments given to various types of financing, plus the public perception of risk attached to share investment. In this latter sense, no one can raise equity capital if the public is unwilling to purchase shares for fear of the risks involved. And in the last several years, the options markets have helped to ameliorate risk by providing share investors with instruments to hedge their risks. Thus, the capital markets' success can only be aided by the hedging markets.

Although this discussion covers the six major financial markets, it cannot, and does not, purport to be comprehensive in the strictest sense of the word. It intends only to give the reader a basic understanding of the nature and function of each market, the fundamentals employed and some timely topics pertaining to them. The medieval philosopher, William of Ockham, devised a method eight centuries ago, which can be of great help in describing financial market phenomena. His basic dictum, known as Ockham's Razor, stated that one should never postulate more than necessary to prove a point. Unnecessary discussions are only tangential to a basic description and, therefore, have been omitted here. Hopefully, this will provide the reader, and especially the introductory level reader, with a foundation unencumbered with superfluous material. Of course, the problem when applying Ockham's Razor is that it is possible to shave the subject too close.

Each financial market has its own set of rules, methods and factors affecting it and these are described in general terms herein. Insofar as possible, general trends such as interest rate movements and their effect upon the markets individually, have been discussed but it should be kept in mind that reactions can only be discussed in the broadest terms possible. Contrary to what the markets themselves may indicate at times, simple cause and effect cannot be taken for granted because of constantly changing international monetary policies and economic conditions.

In this respect, the reader should be aware that text-book generalisations, as they apply to these markets, are used for descriptive, pedagogical purposes only. An example taken from the tumultuous monetary history of 1980 provides an illustration. The worldwide recession that developed in the spring and summer had a profound and unexpected impact upon the major share and bond markets. In the United States, the bond markets staged a huge rally as prices rebounded from historically low levels as soon as it became apparent that the recession had set into the economy. The major factor that triggered this was a decline in interest rates from historically high levels, a phenomenon normally expected when a recession occurs as commercial borrowing slows down. Based upon previous experience, the stock market would have been expected to have remained at moderate, if not depressed, levels since it is normally expected that investors only turn to share investment after a recession has taken its toll on corporate profits or when a turn in the economy can be seen. However, in this case, both markets rallied together, eclipsing the notion that they move inversely to each other.

The British markets also behaved somewhat differently from a textbook example during this period. High interest rates, designed to choke off spending, continued to attract foreign funds and sterling remained at high levels against the dollar despite declining economic performance. The government bond (gilt) market remained at stable levels in the wake of high rates despite the fact that a strong pound was forcing up the price of exports, thereby having a negative impact upon the competitiveness of British industry.

British monetary policy was complicated by the relaxation of what were known as corset controls, imposed on commercial banks in order to curb the level of bank lending. When this sanction was lifted in the spring of 1980, the money supply (M3) increased dramatically as funds which had been lent outside this stricture found their way back into the money stock again. As a result, interest rates had to be maintained at high levels for longer than expected, although the recession began taking its toll on the economy. Throughout this period, the London stock market held up well, supported by foreign interest in certain industrial sectors.

The porous nature of simple cause and effect thinking should also be understood in the context of the two very different types of psychology prevalent in all the markets, namely short-term trading psychology and longer-term investment psychology. The former is much more publicised in the financial press and can be quite bewildering to anyone not familiar with the distinction between them. Short-term trading is geared for *fast* profit and is extremely reactionary in nature. It applies to all markets but can perhaps best be seen in commodity and foreign exchange markets where even one piece of minor news from a remote part of the globe can have an immediate impact upon prices as traders take positions accordingly.

Investing for the longer term, while obviously affected by these short-term, momentary price movements, will overlook what appeared to be minor events and centre instead upon economic fundamentals, both of the financial instrument involved and of the market and economy in which it trades. Certainly, as an investment strategy, it also seeks to maximise trading profits but does not react to events in the same fashion as trading psychology, unless the short-term strategy itself becomes a trend. The obvious difference between the two ultimately lies in the nature of the investor and this will be emphasised in general terms in each chapter.

One additional factor, much more difficult to qualify than perhaps any other, affecting all the financial markets, is the impact of international flows of funds in to and out of domestic economies. Immediately after the second world war this would not have been considered much of an influence due to the fact that many industrialised European countries imposed exchange controls in one form or other to protect their badly damaged economies from outside interference. Within the last decade, however, most vestiges of controls have disappeared and the international flow of money in search of high interest rates and other investment opportunities has increased; in many cases having serious consequences on domestic money stocks and money market rates.

In many cases, these 'hot money' flows provide a curious international view of an economy which may not coincide with its domestic performance. Thus· it is not inconceivable that productivity may be declining and unemployment rising while the currency actually gains strength on the foreign exchange markets, because the money and bond markets attract short-term investment as a result of high interest rates, as was the case of Britain in 1980. These conditions can reach into all other financial markets as well as affecting the ability to raise capital for long-term investment, thereby having a domino effect upon investor behaviour and the perception of risk.

The underlying reason for many of these static ideas, which have characterised the markets for many years, falling by the wayside is the several rounds of OPEC oil price rises since 1974, casting the international financial system into confusion. The doubling of the price of oil has had an immediate ripple effect by inflating prices worldwide. One of these effects has been a hitherto unexperienced price volatility in traditionally conservative financial markets, notably the bond markets. At one time, they were renowned for their price stability *vis-à-vis* stock and commodity markets. Unfortunately, this is no longer the case.

In the discussion of the structure and functions of the markets contained here, the reader will find that some basic terms and concepts will be used in different sectors, and that little distinguishes them except the nuances of the particular market under discussion. Such terms as short-selling, margin trading and hedging do not change their nature from market to market, only their hats and, occasionally, their coats. Therefore, no attempt has been made to re-define them but only to show how they are used in each particular market.

Although this book is divided into two major parts, the following sequence may be of some help to those approaching these markets for the first time. Chapters 1 and 6 (stock and options markets) should be read together as should Chapters 2 and 3 (money and bond markets). Chapter 4 concerning commodities contains the basic theory of hedging while Chapter 5 (foreign exchange) merely expands upon it in discussing a different financial instrument. And although all the chapters are equally important Chapter 1 contains most of the definitions necessary to make the other chapters clearer conceptually.

1 Stock Markets

Stock markets are the best known and perhaps the least understood of all financial markets. They have been decried as punting havens for the rich and as gambling casinos where great fortunes are made and lost. Their general notoriety among the public, even among those who have never owned a share, stems from the fact that their performance, as measured by an index or average, is normally considered one of the prime economic indicators in industrialised economies. As a result, the Dow Jones Averages or the Financial Times Composite Index have become household terms, being widely reported and commented upon by the media.

The economic importance of stock markets has many times been lost in the day to day maze of statistics surrounding them. Their fundamental importance will be emphasised in this chapter many times in different ways but essentially their general importance can be summarised quite succinctly; stock markets provide a pricing mechanism by which companies in need of capital can value themselves, either for the first time or on a continuing basis. The extent to which this function is successful is one of the leading economic indicators as to the health of a national economy. But having said this, other qualifications must be introduced since a falling stock market does not necessarily reflect a flagging economy.

WHAT IS EQUITY?

In the broadest sense, equity is defined as fairness as applied under principles of law. This is its most common meaning, universally recognised. However, the word equity obviously has another derivative meaning in the financial markets; equity is a term synonymous with stock or a share. How did this term become used in such a fashion? The answer lies in the fundamental distinction between owner and creditor, how their particular interests are treated on a company balance sheet, and the rights and protections afforded by law to each.

On a company's balance sheet the liability column will show two distinct categories – *shareholders' equity* and *debt*. These two are the sources of the company's capital structure but there is a fundamental distinction between them. A shareholder is an owner of the company while a debtor (note or bond holder) has lent the company money in return for interest payments. They are treated differently under law. Equity investors as owners are entitled to participate in the company's profits, in the form of dividends (if these are declared) and may also participate in certain activities of the company such as voting for members of the board of directors. Creditors, having lent the company money through a bond purchase (on new issue only) are only entitled to receive interest and the principal of their loan back upon redemption. Both positions are protected by law. For instance, in the event the company declared bankruptcy, creditors must be reimbursed first since equity is subordinated to debt for legal purposes. Only after this has been accomplished can the legal owners divide up what is left by selling off fixed assets or other tangible assets.

Share equity has been a familiar form of ownership in industrial societies since before the Industrial Revolution. It enables a company to accomplish two objectives: by selling shares it is able to expand its capital base while at the same time spreading out the risk of doing business. In this latter respect, this is an advantage of 'going public'; that is, selling shares in what formerly was a private company. By doing so, the original owners of the firm, initially liable for the risks of the business, may incorporate and bring in additional owners. Each new shareholder's ultimate risk under this arrangement is the amount he or she paid for the number of shares owned.

For assuming this risk, the shareholder is, as mentioned, protected by law. Just as the original owner mitigated his original liability by incorporating, the new shareholder is also limited in this new liability. Shareholders are not responsible for a company's managerial decisions and ensuing actions nor are they responsible for the company's debt. Thus, their newly acquired risk is actually a market risk; the amount of their investment will only be affected by price movements of their holdings in the stock market.

The appeal of equity as an investment is based upon several interconnecting factors. First, the investor must believe that the particular company will return a rate better than that he could receive elsewhere, whether it be in other equities or in alternative instruments. Second, regardless of the potential of any particular company, the stock market and economic climate must be conducive to share price appreciation. And third, the investor and the company must understand these factors in order to best utilise market conditions to their mutual advantage.

Since equity is subordinated to debt it is by its nature a more risky investment than bonds. This risk is reflected in price movements on the stock exchanges although it would be incorrect to assume that bond prices have not at times been more highly volatile than shares. However, given the intrinsic nature of shares one may assume, although only in general, that the fortunes of a particular company will be fully and quickly reflected in the share price. It is this general characteristic which makes shares suitable investments for some while carrying too much risk for others.

THE PROFILE OF A SHARE

In order to best understand what both companies themselves and investors search for when examining corporate performance, the profile of a share will be outlined here, discussing the salient features determining its corporate and stock market performance. But the characteristics listed below should not be taken as inclusive; they are only the better known guidelines by which performance is measured. In themselves they do not give a complete picture of a corporation but only illustrate the type of fundamental analysis which leads to further in-depth examination.

Stock markets value shares differently, depending upon a variety of factors relating to the economy in question. But absolute market price is not an indicator of comparative value unless other variables are brought alongside it. For example, imagine two companies in the same business whose shares trade actively on the stock exchange. One is priced at $10 per share while the other is $15. It would be incorrect to assume on this basis that the $15 share is preferable to the $10 share.

In order to fully appreciate market price in a comparative sense one must take into account the *capitalisation* of the companies in question. This is defined as the amount derived by multiplying the current market price by the number of shares outstanding. It is possible that these two companies are capitalised the same at current prices. For instance,

Company 1:   capitalisation = market price per share × number
                                of shares outstanding
                                or
             $15 000 000   = $10 × 1 500 000
Company 2:   capitalisation = market price per share × number
                                of shares outstanding
                                or
             $15 000 000   = $15 × 1 000 000

Assume that we are examining the finances of a hypothetical company. On its balance sheet we see that it has 1 million shares 'authorised and outstanding'; that is, the amount of shares in the hands of the public is also the same number the company is authorised to issue.[1] This figure is extremely important because it will be a constant *numéraire* when employing certain measures to examine the company's performance.[2] The above illustration is one example.

The *earnings* of a company may be quoted on a pre or after tax basis but normally it is the after tax figure that is of most importance to the financial analyst. However, on its own the amount is of little relevance unless compared with figures from previous years. And the market also sets this figure against estimates for the year made by both the company and financial analysts and commentators. A 10 per cent increase in earnings may be quite good for companies in some industries while being poor for others.

Earnings are derived by subtracting the costs of doing business from revenues. Included in these costs is the category of interest expense; that is, the amount of money paid out to creditors during that tax year. This expense is deducted from revenues even before earnings before tax are stated. This underscores a point made in the previous section; equity is subordinated to debt and they are treated quite differently on a company's profit and loss statement as well as on the balance sheet.

Earnings per share, or eps, is perhaps the most important single indicator watched in the stock markets since it succinctly states the measure of a company's performance. It is defined as earnings divided by number of outstanding shares. But as already mentioned, absolute levels of any figure can be meaningless unless used in a comparative framework. The stock market measure by which companies in an industry group are compared to each other is called the *price/earnings ratio*, or pe. This is derived by simply dividing the current market price of the stock by the eps. This is also sometimes referred to as the pe multiple. Pes are extremely important when compared to each other.

For example, an examination of stocks within a specific industry group might reveal that the average pe for the group was 10. An investor might find an individual within the group with a pe of only 6. In market terms, the shares are undervalued in relation to the group. It then becomes a matter of discerning the reason why.

Earnings are also important in determining the *dividend* of the company; the amount paid out to the shareholders. Therefore, the investor uses the dividends as one measure of his own personal return on equity. The level of dividends paid out tends to vary according to the industry group of the company. Some industry groups, such as public utilities in the United States, are noted for the high dividend paid out on their shares. Others, notably those companies in high technology areas tend to pay out less if anything at all, preferring to use the money for research and development or increased capital costs. Thus dividends, or the lack of them, are not an indication of the financial health of a company. However, a change in the dividend rate is often taken as an indicator of changing company fortunes. An omitted dividend is often taken to mean that a company's earnings prospects have declined.

The dividend yield is normally stated in percentage terms and is calculated by dividing the dividend per share by the current market price of the stock. A stock with a dividend of 50 cents and a market price of $10 thus yields

$$\frac{0.50}{10.00} = 5\%$$

Dividends paid are treated as ordinary income by most domestic tax authorities. By virtue of this fact, they have at times also borne the brunt of economic controls. Dividend controls *per se* were instituted in Britain in 1973 and were only rescinded in 1979. The intention of the authorities in controlling dividends was to control inflation by limiting the amount of money paid out to shareholders. This had the net effect of raising the *dividend cover* of many British companies; that is, it reduced the amount available for dividend payout and therefore raised the number of times earnings per share covered dividends per share (eps/dps).

Shares are rated as to quality by various international rating services although the American agencies give perhaps the most visible or widely disseminated classifications of domestic and select international issues. The agencies employ different financial models in their rating processes but essentially they break down their quality categories in a similar

TABLE 1.1   US equity ratings by agency (common stocks)

Standard & Poor's	Moody's	description
A+	high grade	highest rating
A	investment grade	high rating
A−	upper medium grade	above average
B+	medium grade	average rating
B	lower medium grade	below average
B−	–	lower than average
C	speculative grade	–
D	–	reorganisation

manner. Table 1.1 lists the classifications employed by the two major American agencies. These categories can have a profound impact upon investor attitudes and the subsequent price behaviour of shares. For instance, a stock rating which falls from A to B+ will probably suffer a drop in market price to reflect the higher risk now attached since the rating fall suggests a declining financial position; not necessarily in terms of sales or revenues but of a deterioration in the company's overall financial health. This situation can also lead to an additional cost of capital if new equity is to be raised in the future.

THE EQUITY RAISING PROCESS

The amount of equity employed in a company's financial structure is a combination of the actual cost of equity versus debt to the firm plus an element of tradition as well. The traditional aspect derives from the nature of the investment banking function in the particular country where the company is located. For example, the average debt/equity ratio (total debt outstanding/equity from all sources) in the United States (non-financial companies) is about 50 per cent, or 1 : 1, and it is about the same in Britain. However, in other countries it can be much higher due to the fact that banks play a more central role in providing funds to corporations than do equity shareholders. Thus, in Japan, debt/equity ratios can be as high as 4 : 1 or more. The amount of equity employed depends to a great extent upon the acceptance shares have gained historically with the investing public. The amount of personal savings households, or individuals, are likely to invest in equities depends upon a multiplicity of factors, many of which can be difficult to qualify. But perhaps the most fundamental is the return that equities have yielded historically over bonds and other forms of investment. Many times this perception is not based upon empirical evidence in so far as the public is concerned but upon price volatility of shares themselves. An investor who purchased shares at $10 in year one, finding them at $10 in year five, knows full well that he might have done better elsewhere, especially if his dividend yield has not changed over that period. The investors' aggregate reaction will eventually be felt by all of those involved in financing, whether in equities or a competing sector.

Assume that a company is contemplating a new equity issue. It is a high technology company currently paying a dividend of 2 per cent. In order to successfully market the shares, the company must be able to maintain its dividend to cover the number of new shares.

This cost must be compared with the interest that would have to be paid on a new bond issue. If the company is well rated on both its equity and bond issues outstanding then its cost of capital should fall within the accepted range for issues currently outstanding in the market. If we assume that the current bond yield for such a company is 10 per cent then the large differential in the cost of the two funds militates heavily in favour of equity.

But the decision to choose equity in this instance rests equally upon other factors. The attitude of the stock market is a crucial factor here. If the market is unreceptive to high technology shares at this moment or if the shares are trading at a low pe then an equity issue would not be advantageous. Generally, companies of this nature find it beneficial to make new issues when their shares are high, ensuring themselves of more new capital than if the shares were priced low. The gearing (or leverage) aspect also enters here. If the company found that it could not increase its debt/equity ratio by 5 per cent in favour of debt without affecting its market position adversely then the choice of equity would prove a viable alternative.[3]

The actual methods of issuing shares differ from market to market, depending upon local practice and banking structure. They will be dealt with individually below in the section on individual markets. Aside from new issues *per se*, several other methods exist of issuing additional shares which are common both to the United States and Britain.

One method of marketing future new shares, affording the investor the potential of capital gain, is the issuance of debentures, or bonds, with warrants attached. These warrants entitle the holder to x number of shares, converted at a specific market price. Since the acquisition of the new shares in the future is contingent upon acquiring debt of the company, the firm is able to achieve a double objective by issuing two types of instrument rather than choosing one or the other. The advantage to the holder is that the bond cannot be called in at the time of warrant exercise (unlike a convertible bond which retires upon exercise when it is converted into shares). The potential for capital gain also exists because the shares might well be above exercise price come conversion day.

A second method of issuing new shares, avoiding a public offering, is the *scrip issue* (in UK terms) or *stock dividend* (in US terms). This type offers existing shareholders new stock as dividend payment rather than cash. A company may decide that in lieu of a cash dividend it may offer fractional shares instead. This can save it cash flow while yet expanding its capital base. If successful, this type of operation will increase both the total capitalisation of the company and the number of shares outstanding. If each investor received 3 shares for each 100 he held, then the equity value has increased by 3 per cent, assuming that the price of the shares hold up in the market. The investor who decides to sell the new shares or take cash instead (if this option is available) reduces his overall holding in the company by 3 per cent.

Similar in some respects to a scrip issue is a *rights issue* whereby existing shareholders are offered new shares at a specified offering price, in proportion to the number of shares already held. Several options normally present themselves here to the investor. In addition to subscribing to the issue, he may subscribe and then sell the rights separately or may sell the shares with the rights still attached. If the shareholder should decline the offer entirely, then his holding in the company will decline by the percentage of the rights offering itself.

Another method of increasing the number of shares outstanding is known as a *stock split*. Splits may be in any proportion that the company desires. Usually, an announcement is made that on a certain date a specific fractional division of shares will occur. A 2 for 1 split means that each holder of 1 share will hold 2; the number of shares outstanding will be increased 100 per cent.

On the day of the split, the stock market will react by marking down the price of the shares by 50 per cent. Shares originally selling at x will now be priced at $\frac{1}{2}x$. In short, the number of shares outstanding has increased but the total capitalisation of the company remains unchanged.

Why would a company decide to split its shares? Normally, their market price is the underlying reason. If share prices begin to reach heights (regardless of pe) that the company felt were a hindrance to investor psychology and concomitantly to the issue of new shares at that price then a split would become desirable. Shares at $150 or £20 are less appealing psychologically than they are after a 5 for 1 split at $30 and £4 respectively.

So far we have discussed methods of increasing the number of shares outstanding but it should be noted that companies occasionally do purchase shares in the market in order to reduce the amount in the hands of the general public. Many times this operation is carried out to provide shares for internal corporate purposes although there can be more strategic corporate reasons for doing so. But regardless of the purpose, once shares are bought in they are effectively retired and become known as *treasury stock*. Such stock is retired with cash which normally would have been used to pay dividends. Besides reducing the number outstanding, this operation boosts the eps of the company and this can affect market price. It should be noted that this procedure is an American practice which is forbidden in Britain by the Companies Act.

PREFERENCE SHARES

Thus far we have been describing what are known as *ordinary shares* (in British parlance) or *common stock* (in American parlance). However, there is another category of shares which are akin to both ordinary stock and fixed income securities, known as preference (Britain) or preferred (United States) shares. These instruments have a stated amount of dividend paid, normally expressed in percentage terms. In this respect, they are closely allied with fixed income securities, in that they normally appeal to fixed-income minded investors. In other respects, they are more akin to ordinary shares. Dividends on preference shares cannot be changed by the issuing company; once they have been fixed on initial distribution they remain fixed. But unlike debt, preference dividends are still treated as dividends on the balance sheet and are subordinated to debt. Thus, if a company's profitability is hurt, dividends on both ordinary and preferred shares can be reduced.

These instruments may have other additional features attached to them as well.[4] They may be convertible into ordinary shares of the company and may also be cumulative. This means that if a dividend is omitted, the missed payment will be made up by the company when its financial health improves. From the investors' point of view these many features can enhance the shares' attraction. This can be especially true in times of interest rate unrest when an additional element of risk is added to them. If interest rates rise, the shares will fall to a discount since their return is fixed. This exposes them to another risk in addition to the normal risk of the company doing business. A feature such as a cumulative option may help to allay investor fears and be instrumental in marketing the shares.

CONCEPTS AND FUNDAMENTAL TECHNIQUES

To many who approach stock markets for the first time, their terminology, concepts and techniques appear as if the world was turned upside down. The very idea that someone may sell something he does not own, purchase it later at a lower price and make a profit does appear somewhat alien at first glance if not downright illegal. However, these somewhat peculiarly illogical concepts form the basis of all financial market techniques and will be discussed in the other chapters as well.

The simplest of all market operations is the purchase of securities; in market patois this is known as 'going long' or assuming a *long position*. Selling securities does not have any argot peculiar to it but a variation – *short selling* – is a practice requiring further explanation. This occurs when an investor sells a security he does not own. The only way that money can be made through such a transaction is when the security is later purchased at a lower price. This is called *short covering*; that is, closing the short sale by purchasing the same security.[5] This is shown diagrammatically in Figure 1.1.

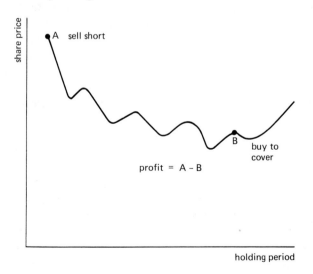

FIGURE 1.1   Short selling

This technique is used by investors who believe that certain securities are overpriced and likely to depreciate in the near future. They then sell the security in the hope that it will fall, making them a profit on the way down. Short selling is a difficult activity to gauge since short sales are recorded as normal selling transactions in so far as everyday public recording is concerned. It is not possible to read the daily transactions of a particular share in a newspaper and determine if any shares have been shorted. However, short sales on the major exchanges in the United States are recorded and reported once per month in what is known as the *short interest* list. This shows the outstanding number of shares shorted for each stock. The term interest here has nothing to do with money paid on a loan but merely means the amount of shares attracting short selling interest.

Short selling is a popular device used by knowledgeable equity investors and is even more popular in the commodity markets (see Chapter 4). Another market technique common to all the financial markets – *arbitrage* – also uses short selling frequently as a tool. Arbitrage is the method whereby an investor buys a security in one market and simultaneously sells it in another market, when legally able to do so. Arbitrage techniques differ from stock market to stock market but traditionally they have been confined to two or more markets which happen to trade the same security, for instance the New York and Pacific Stock Exchanges or the London and Sydney exchanges. The process is very rapid and is based upon even the smallest of price differentials. It has also been extended to imply transactions involving the buying and selling of securities in the same security classification but not actually the same security. The theory behind this type of intra-industry arbitrage can be very difficult to grasp but a return to a point made earlier may help to elucidate the concept.

Assume that an industry group contains five companies, all of which have similar capital structures and credit ratings (Table 1.2). They all

TABLE 1.2   Intra-industry arbitrage

company number	debt/equity ratio	rating	eps	market price	pe
1	1 : 1	A	$1	$10	10
2	1 : 1	A	$2	$20	10
3	1 : 1	A	$3	$24	8
4	1 : 1	A	$4	$40	10
5	1 : 1	A	$5	$50	10

have similar earnings and pay out similar dividends. Therefore, they should all have the same pe ratio. But in this hypothetical group, the pe of stock 3 is lower than the others and is therefore currently undervalued. The question is this – does switching out of the other stocks into stock 3 to take advantage of this price differential constitute arbitrage? Put another way, does the investor stand to gain through what appears to be a riskless transaction?

The answer is yes here, assuming that all other internal and external factors remain equal. If company 3's earnings were to decline, jeopardising the dividend, or it were to incur extraordinary losses then the investor is actually assuming an additional risk for which the lower share price may not compensate.

When using the term arbitrage in this book we will use it in its strict sense; normally it will be used to imply either one of the techniques described above. The simple criterion used here will be that any security substituted for another must be a comparable economic substitute; that is, it must be in the same risk category and must also return a similar payment in dividend (or interest) to the investor.

Perhaps one of the least understood techniques used in trading securities is *margin trading*. This is the technique of buying securities on credit, as extended by either the brokerage house or bank involved as agent in the transaction. Margin trading is quite common in the United States and to a lesser extent on the Continent but currently is not practised in Britain.

This method allows the investor to gear up or leverage himself in order to buy shares, usually for a fraction of the purchase or selling price involved. One hundred shares of a stock selling at $50 could then be purchased (or sold short) for $2500 rather than $5000, assuming a margin requirement of 50 per cent. The debit balance is charged interest at a money market rate, known in the US as the *broker loan rate*. Usually, this rate is $1-1\frac{1}{2}$ per cent below the US prime rate charged by banks and as such is a primary indicator in gauging the course of the prime itself. Also, little known outside the investment community is the effect that the broker loan rate can have upon the general level of prices on the US exchanges.

It is normally assumed that higher interest rates have a negative effect upon shares by eroding corporate profits and concomitantly eroding stock prices as risk to the company under such a regime increases. But rising interest rates have an equally profound and more immediate impact by creating what is known as a *margin shake-out*. As rates rise, the costs of carrying shares on margin becomes more expensive and many positions will be liquidated rather than continue financing the shares. Thus, share prices may erode in this manner although nothing has happened to change the fundamental economic profile of a company.

In subsequent chapters, the general effects of rising interest rates upon specific financial markets will be discussed. It is noteworthy, however, that some of the traditional generalisations about the effect of higher rates, as well as other economic phenomena, will change in the future due to the inflationary spiral experienced in 1979–80. Prior to the mid-1970s, general opinion held that increases in the money supply (normally M1) suggested an upsurge in share prices as more money became available for potential stock investment. At the same time, it was also assumed that bond prices moved inversely with the money supply; that is, an increase in M1 would lead to a decrease in bond prices. Thus, the general syllogism held that stock and bond prices also moved in an inverse relationship. Although this latter statement is still generally true and proved by price behaviour in the various markets, the increasing popularity of monetary theory in both Britain and America has led to the demise of the first theory, namely that more money stock was good medicine for the stock markets.

The ever-growing emphasis upon monetarism has led to the newly formulated notion that an expanding money supply creates a demand pull inflation which is inimical to rising stock prices because it debases savings and corporate profits. While the theory is certainly not new, the emphasis upon the relationship between the quantity of the money stock and share performance has come to the fore in the last several years and now has become almost a shibboleth among many market professionals. Whether or not many of the convenient aphorisms the markets use will endure is not of primary importance here but it should be remembered that when coupled with market fundamentals and jargon they can become very impressive arguments which may or may not necessarily reflect the actual condition of the markets' health or direction.

AMERICAN STOCK MARKETS

When one speaks of the American stock markets it is normally assumed that the New York Stock Exchange (NYSE) is meant exclusively. However, the two names are not necessarily interchangeable because the NYSE is quite distinct from the other stock exchanges and the over-the-counter market. Despite the fact that over 80% of all stock exchange transactions take place on the NYSE, the other national and regional markets nevertheless provide an equally valuable service in the pricing and trading of equities.

Since its inception in 1792, the NYSE has experienced a multiplicity of changes. In 1830, it suffered the dullest day in its then short history as only 31 shares were traded. The crash of 1929 saw a record 16 million shares change hands and, more recently in 1978, a new one day record was established when 65 million shares traded. And perhaps one of the most fundamental and potentially significant events for all the exchanges occurred in 1974 when a consolidated price reporting system was instituted whereby all equity trades, regardless of exchange locale, are reported on the same ticker tape system.

In addition to the NYSE, the American Stock Exchange (Amex) is the other national exchange trading shares. Currently, the Amex accounts for some 9–10 per cent of the national total (see Table 1.3), the other exchanges – Boston, Philadelphia, Midwest, Pacific – accounting for the remaining 10 per cent between them. The basic difference between the NYSE and the Amex is the capitalisation of the companies traded. Generally, companies on the NYSE have larger total capitalisations than those on the Amex. The difference between the national exchanges and the regionals is more subtle. For the most part, the regional exchanges trade those shares already listed on either the NYSE or Amex which have a local appeal, either through locale of the company or through some other historical relationship.

Before the consolidated tape, it was possible to arbitrage shares between American exchanges. Although prices of dually listed shares moved in tandem, inter day price anomalies did occasionally appear which traders could take advantage of. It was possible to buy shares on one exchange and simultaneously sell them on another. After the consolidated reporting system was instituted this practice became more

TABLE 1.3   US Stock Exchange volume (1979)*
(in 000)

exchange	total	%
New York Stock Exchange	8 675 253	79.9
American Stock Exchange	1 161 325	10.7
others	1 026 209	9.4

* Gross numbers of shares bought and sold.
SOURCE: New York Stock Exchange, *Fact Book* 1980.

TABLE 1.4　Capitalisation of major stock exchanges (end year 1979) (£ millions)

exchange	total market value	number of equities listed
NYSE*	666 127	2 200
UK	211 301	2 700
Tokyo*	210 428	1 300
Paris	81 369	na
Geneva & Zurich*	69 243	na
Brussels	30 011	na

* value of equities only. na = not available
SOURCE: London Stock Exchange, *Fact Book* 1980

difficult due to the fact that all traders then had access to the same price information at the same time.

Despite several periods of poor or mediocre performance in recent years, the NYSE remains the world's largest stock market in terms of total capitalisation; that is, the total number of shares outstanding of all companies listed times their current market prices. Comparative figures with other stock markets can be found in Table 1.4. As can be seen, the London Stock Exchange trades more shares of more listed companies than does New York but the total capitalisation is still smaller.

The Mechanics of Share Trading

Share performance in the United States is measured by several indices, or averages; among them are the Dow Jones Industrial Average (of 30 leading industrial companies), the Dow Jones Transportation and Utilities Averages, the New York Stock Exchange All Common Index and the Standard and Poor's 500 Common Stock Average. Of this group, the Dow Jones Industrial Average remains the most widely used reporting average although it is less broadly based than some of the other indicators. The market's overall performance forms one of the Commerce Department's leading economic indicators and is, in the opinion of many, the premier indicator of this basket of economic signals.

The actual mechanics of share trading bear some examination here both for simple information purposes and for more far-reaching social reasons as well. In this latter respect, how shares are traded and the public's perception of the efficiency of the stock markets has been the focal point for much discussion concerning institutional domination of the stock markets, a topic discussed more fully later in this section. But before these implications can be treated, a few basic methods should be elaborated upon.

Actual trading on the exchanges is broken into two ordinary categories – even and odd lot orders. Even lots are those of 100 shares or multiples thereof. Odd lots are literally anything else. Regardless of the size of an order, stocks trade in dollars and fractions of dollars rather than in cents. A share trading at 30 means \$30 while $30\frac{1}{8}$ means \$30.125.[6] The smallest fraction used in quoting listed stocks is normally $\frac{1}{8}$. When a spread is quoted, such as $30–30\frac{1}{4}$, it simply means that you may buy the shares at $30\frac{1}{4}$ or sell at 30. The difference is the profit kept by the trader who maintains the auction market on the floor of the exchange.

All stock exchanges operate on an auction system where bids and offers are made through a central broker(s) on the exchange floor. On the American exchanges, this central broker is known as a *specialist* and he is entrusted with a twofold duty. In addition to executing all primary orders on behalf of other brokers and maintaining a market, the specialist also trades for his own account (he does not deal directly with the public). This is a function distinctly different from the *market maker* system used in the United States (see under Over-the-Counter section below) but quite similar to the *jobbing system* used in Britain in that it allows one individual both functions.

Larger orders of shares, larger than those considered ordinary orders (*c.* 5000 shares or more), are referred to as *block trades*. These high volume trades may be handled by a specialist on an exchange floor or may be accomplished by bringing buyer and seller together off the floor in what is known as a *secondary distribution*. Currently, block trades account for some 20–25 per cent of all NYSE transactions.

An example of a newspaper quotation puts much of this share terminology in perspective and also utilises some terms previously introduced. In Table 1.5 it can be seen that the year's high/low for shares is listed along with their current price, dividend yield, pe, and volume traded.

Although the above quoted price information gives volume information it does not reflect the structural nature of trading volume itself. This problem brings the nature of the specialist system and trading patterns into focus and helps us centre upon one of the NYSE's major debating points in recent years. Within the last ten years as much as 70–75 per cent of business originated on the exchanges has been

TABLE 1.5 US and UK Stock Market quotations

US

12 Month High	12 Month Low	Stock	Div.	Yld.	P/E	Sls. 100s.	High	Low	Close Quot.	Ch'ge Prev Close
53⅝	36⅛	Interco	2.64	5.4	7	568	49½	48¾	48¾	— ½
116	81	Inter pf	7.75	7.2		10	107	107	107	— ½
33¾	22½	Intrlk	2.20	7.8	21	45	28¼	28¼	28¼	— ¼
16⅜	9½	IntAlu	.60	4.7	5	27	13	12¾	12¾	— ¼
72¾	50⅜	IBM	3.44	5.2	12	8404	67	65¾	66¾	+ 1
27½	16⅝	IntFlav	.92	4.2	12	225	22	21¼	21⅞	+ ⅜
35½	22⅛	IntHarv	1.20	5.2		579	23½	23	23¼	
49¼	40⅛	IntHr pf	5.76	13.		58	46½	45⅛	45¾	— ¼
66½	30¼	IntMn	s 2.32	3.9	10	160	59¾	58⅞	59	— ¼
20⅞	13¼	IntMult	1.32	6.9	8	42	19½	19¼	19¼	— ½
47⅞	30½	IntPapr	2.40	5.6	7	250	43⅛	42⅜	42⅝	— ⅛
30¾	16⅜	IntRect	.32	1.7	6	23	18¾	18½	18¾	+ ⅛
33⅞	22⅞	IntTT	2.60	8.6	6	625	30½	29¾	30¼	
55½	38½	ITT pfJ	4	8.1		8	49⅝	49½	49⅝	— ⅞
53⅜	36¼	ITT pfK	4	8.4		23	48	47⅝	47⅝	— ¾
52⅞	40	ITT pfO	5	11.		2	47¼	46¾	47¼	+ 1
41⅝	29	IntTT pf	2.25	6.0		11	37⅞	37⅝	37⅝	— ¼
56	38⅝	IntTT pf	4.50	9.0		6	50	50	50	
49¾	26⅛	IntNth	s1.80	4.5	8	230	40¼	39¾	39¾	
97¼	88⅝	IntNt pf	8.48	9.5		z170	89	89	89	+ ⅛
31¼	18¼	Intrpce	1.50	7.4	8	40	20⅜	20	20⅜	+ ⅜
14⅞	10½	IntstPw	1.56	13.	7	8	12⅝	12⅜	12⅜	— ⅛
49	22¼	IowaBf	.70	1.5	9	249	47⅜	47	47⅜	+ ⅜
14½	11	IowaEl	1.66	13.	6	31	12¾	12⅜	12⅝	— ⅛
20⅝	14⅝	IowIIG	2.20	13.	7	39	17¼	16⅝	17¼	+ ½
22⅛	16½	IowaPS	2.20	11.	7	14	19¼	19	19¼	+ ¼
24⅞	18½	IowaRs	2.72	12.	6	15	22⅜	22	22	— ¼
6⅛	3½	IpcoCp	.12	2.3		259	5¼	5	5⅛	+ ⅜
49¼	30	IrvgBk	2.72	5.6	5	47	49¼	48⅜	48⅜	— ⅜
35¾	16⅜	ItekCp	.15e	.4	19	320	34½	33¾	33⅞	— ½

UK

1980-81 High	1980-81 Low	Stock	Price	+ or —	Div. Net	C'vr	Y'ld Gr's	P/E
600	295	Akzo Fl.20	350	......	—	—	—	—
138	84	All'd Colloid 10p .	119	−3	2.54	2.1	3.0	(18.2)
88	55	Anchor Chem. ..	68	−1	5.3	2.1	11.1	(5.0)
116	20	Arrow Chemicals.	38	−1	1.4	1.8	5.3	15.8
£36¼	£23½	BASF AG DM50 .	£26½	......	Q16%	2.1	6.4	7.4
£32½	£21½	Bayer AG. DM.50	£23⅝	......	Q21.88%	1.3	9.9	7.8
132	86	Blagden Noakes..	102	......	6.0	ϕ	8.7	ϕ
*163	115	Brent Chems 10p.	147	−2	†4.5	2.9	4.4	16.8
55	18	Brit. Benzol 10p..	22½	......	‡2.0	—	‡	—
41	21	Brit. Tar Prd. 10p.	26	......	h2.1	3.0	11.5	3.3
82	44	Catalin............	49	......	3.85	3.2	11.2	4.0
£101	£91	CibaG'gy 7¼% Ln.	£101	......	Q7¼%	ϕ	f7.2	—
£88	£80	Do.8%Cnv81/94.	£87½	......	Q8%	ϕ	f9.5	—
£86½	£78½	Do.8¼%Cnv.82/95..	£85	......	Q8¼%	ϕ	f10.1	—
*146	82	Coalite Group...	121	−2	†3.85	4.4	4.5	6.1
63	47	Coates Bros......	47	......	♠3.0	3.1	9.1	4.6
62	46	Do. 'A' NV......	44	......	♠3.0	3.1	9.3	4.5
21½	15	Cory (Horace) 5p	15½	+½	1.3	2.5	12.4	3.9
54	32	Croda Int. 10p..	34	−½	3.1	2.8	13.6	(2.9)
29	17	Croda Int. Defd.	20	......	—	—	—	—
36	14	Dixor-Strand 5p..	15	−1	—	—	—	—
144	108	Ellis & Everard.	122	......	6.5	1.4	7.6	13.3
304	112	Fisons £1	130	−3	10.0	—	11.2	—
46½	27	Halstead (J.) 10p	41	+1	2.4	3.7	8.7	3.7
180	132	Hksn. Welch 50p.	149	+1	7.5	2.3	7.2	8.8
322	223	Hoechst DM5...	247	+2	tQ21.9%	2.1	9.4	5.0

institutional in nature rather than retail (from individual investors). The essential difference between the two is the size in which shares are bought and sold. Although there is no single threshold in terms of volume, institutional trading activity can be generally determined by the level of individual investor interest, in part as measured by various investing surveys, and the volatility of share prices on the exchanges.

The amount of institutional trading on the stock exchanges is a sensitive indicator of intermediation in the financial markets. What this means is really quite simple: interest in shares on the part of the individual investor has waned and he thus places his investment funds elsewhere, seeking a tolerably high return. If we assume that he places them with an institution of one sort or another (mutual fund for example) committed to the same sort of growth return he desires, then the money will again be placed in the stock markets, with one major difference; this time it is the institution doing the investing rather than the individual. The more individuals contributing to this intermediation the more power the institutional investor accrues and the more influence it is likely to have upon share prices. In short, ten individual orders to purchase 100 shares each are less likely to have a volatile effect on prices than one order of 1000 shares.

According to the NYSE, between 1970 and 1975 total share investors declined by some $5\frac{1}{2}$ million individuals. Between 1975 and 1980, the total number of individual investors returned to its pre-1970 level of approximately thirty million but the actual value of the individual's portfolio declined by approximately fifty per cent. Therefore a net loss was still suffered in money, if not in investor, terms. Yet despite the flight of the small investor, due in no small part to the recession of 1974, trading volume on the exchanges increased during the 1970s overall. The hiatus left by the individual was filled by institutional investors but several qualifications should be made here on this point.

In a public opinion study published in 1978, the NYSE concluded that 54 per cent of households in the United States had never owned a share.[7] This means that the individuals themselves had never owned a share but does not preclude the fact that they may nevertheless have been the indirect owner of shares through a mutual fund, pension fund or the like. Thus, the process of intermediation by institutions on behalf of individuals in some respects accounts for the slack left by the individuals themselves.[8]

The general public attitude against shares is normally reinforced in inflationary or recessionary periods as stock prices begin to tumble and shares become perceived as highly volatile investment instruments. However, the persistence of these notions has equally damaging effects upon the markets. As long as such perceptions linger, other financial instruments will be the net recipients while shares decline in popularity. In another study published in 1975, the NYSE examined the impact of the growth of bonds and other forms of debt upon the capital structures of US corporations and upon the new issues market for shares generally.[9] As can be seen in Table 1.6, shares have undergone a steady

TABLE 1.6　Equity　*v.*　debt　issues　in　US ($ billions)

year	net equity issues	net bond issues
1968	− 1.5	12.9
1969	2.9	12.0
1970	4.8	19.8
1971	11.7	18.8
1972	10.4	12.2
1973	7.2	9.2
1974	3.5	19.0

SOURCE: New York Stock Exchange, *Supply and Demand for Equity Capital*

eclipse in popularity as financing instruments while bonds have grown in corporate and investing popularity. This trend originally stems from the reluctance of the public (this includes many institutional investors as well) to purchase shares, eschewing the risk (real or otherwise) associated with them in favour of medium and long term debt certificates, perceived to be safer instruments.

The increasing institutionalisation of share investing has obvious implications for the behaviour of prices on the exchanges. Large orders can put increasing pressure upon the specialists' capital positions, especially in times of crisis. Prices will tend to gyrate as a result, especially if (for example) one retail purchase of 100 shares were followed by two institutional orders to sell 5000 each. Erratic price movements in either direction then only tend to support a self-fulfilling prophecy on the part of over half the population; stock markets are arenas to be avoided by the small investor since price movements are too volatile to be borne by those with limited capital or background understanding of how to limit risk.

Methods of New Share Issuance

Stock Exchanges in the United States do not actually raise new capital for industry directly. Rather they perform a pricing mechanism whereby new shares can be valued. There is a distinct difference between day-to-day trading on the exchanges *vis-à-vis* the process of bringing new or additional shares into existence.

Earlier in this chapter several methods of adding to the number of shares outstanding were mentioned, all of which were common to the anglophone economies, with slight variations. However, the specific methods used to bring additional large numbers of shares was avoided because, in this one respect, American and British practice tends to differ.

In the United States, two methods exist whereby new shares can come into existence. Both may be classified as a 'new issue' so a further qualification needs to be made. Shares issued for the first time, for what was previously a private company, may be classified as a *primary distribution*. Shares floated in this manner are issued in the over-the-counter market; that is, off the organised exchanges (see next section). Then as their popularity and capitalisation increases they will ultimately be listed on an exchange so that secondary market trading in the shares is more easily facilitated and exposed to the investing public at large.

Primary distributions are therefore a part of what is known as the

All of these Securities have been sold. This announcement appears as a matter of record only.

Not a New Issue

2,650,000 Shares

Getty Oil Company

Common Stock

without par value

MORGAN STANLEY & CO.
Incorporated

LEHMAN BROTHERS KUHN LOEB   **GOLDMAN, SACHS & CO.**   **BLYTH EASTMAN PAINE WEBBER**
Incorporated   *Incorporated*

E. F. HUTTON & COMPANY INC.   **MERRILL LYNCH WHITE WELD CAPITAL MARKETS GROUP**
Merrill Lynch, Pierce, Fenner & Smith Incorporated

ATLANTIC CAPITAL   BACHE HALSEY STUART SHIELDS   BASLE SECURITIES CORPORATION   BEAR, STEARNS & CO.
Corporation   *Incorporated*

DILLON, READ & CO. INC.   **DONALDSON, LUFKIN & JENRETTE**   **DREXEL BURNHAM LAMBERT**
Securities Corporation   *Incorporated*

KIDDER, PEABODY & CO.   **LAZARD FRERES & CO.**   **L. F. ROTHSCHILD, UNTERBERG, TOWBIN**
Incorporated

SHEARSON LOEB RHOADES INC.   **SMITH BARNEY, HARRIS UPHAM & CO.**   **UBS SECURITIES, INC.**
Incorporated

WARBURG PARIBAS BECKER   **WERTHEIM & CO., INC.**   **DEAN WITTER REYNOLDS INC.**
Incorporated

DAIWA SECURITIES AMERICA INC.   EUROPARTNERS SECURITIES CORPORATION   ROBERT FLEMING
Incorporated

KLEINWORT, BENSON   **NEW COURT SECURITIES CORPORATION**
Incorporated

THE NIKKO SECURITIES CO.   **NOMURA SECURITIES INTERNATIONAL, INC.**
International, Inc.

YAMAICHI INTERNATIONAL (AMERICA), INC.   ASSOCIATED EUROPEAN CAPITAL CORPORATION

CAZENOVE INC.   **BAER SECURITIES CORPORATION**

ULTRAFIN INTERNATIONAL CORPORATION   NEW JAPAN SECURITIES INTERNATIONAL INC.

NIPPON KANGYO KAKUMARU INTERNATIONAL, INC.   **SANYO SECURITIES AMERICA INC.**

ALGEMENE BANK NEDERLAND N.V.   **AMSTERDAM-ROTTERDAM BANK N.V.**

BANCA DELLA SVIZZERA ITALIANA   **BANQUE NATIONALE DE PARIS**

BANQUE DE NEUFLIZE, SCHLUMBERGER, MALLET   **CAISSE DES DEPOTS ET CONSIGNATIONS**

COUNTY BANK   **CREDIT COMMERCIAL DE FRANCE**   **HILL SAMUEL & CO.**
Limited   *Limited*

MORGAN GRENFELL & CO.   **SAL. OPPENHEIM JR. & CIE.**   **PICTET INTERNATIONAL**
Limited   *Limited*

SOCIETE GENERALE DE BANQUE S.A.   **VEREINS- UND WESTBANK**   **WESTDEUTSCHE LANDESBANK**
Aktiengesellschaft   **GIROZENTRALE**

November 14, 1980

FIGURE 1.2   Equity tombstone advertisement

primary market; that is, the market for new shares. Whether the discussion of primary market centres around shares or bonds it means, in all cases, the market away from the exchanges.

The second form of share distribution is an addition to shares already outstanding and is called a *secondary distribution*. This is also a new issues market function. It should not be confused with a type of block order mentioned above. Assume that 1 million new shares are being added to 3 million already outstanding and actively traded. At a specific hour, these new shares will be valued and offered to the public at the same price as those already trading. The exchanges do not perform any direct function here; the primary market for secondary distributions is conducted over-the-counter between the issuing investment banking syndicate and the investing public in the over-the-counter markets; that is, via telephone. On a certain date, the new shares are added to the official list of outstanding shares on the respective exchange.

New share issuance is controlled by investment banks rather than commercial banks. The distinction between the two traces back legislatively to the Glass-Steagall Act of 1933 when the process of issuing new securities (by investment banks, for a fee) was divorced from investing in those same securities in fiduciary accounts (a major function of commercial banks). Therefore, the names that appear on a tombstone advertisement (Figure 1.2) will not include the names of any commercial banks but only those of the investment banks and/or brokers who underwrite and distribute them.

The Over-the-Counter Market

Thus far, only the organised stock exchanges themselves have been discussed although mention of the *over-the-counter*, or otc, market has emerged when discussing new issues. The otc market is an integral part of the United States stock market although it is almost totally invisible to the public eye, except for price quotations printed in the newspapers.

The market is a nationwide system or communication network trading the shares of lesser-known companies whose capitalisations are not as large as those of exchange listed companies. Actual trading is conducted by brokers/dealers who maintain markets in the individual shares. The professionals are linked by telephone and by an automated price reporting system, governed by the National Association of Securities Dealers (NASD), empowered to oversee this portion of the profession by the Securities Act of 1933. Although it lacks a central trading location, the otc market is nevertheless efficient in its economic functions.

In addition to trading shares, the otc market also trades the major proportion of bonds sold in the United States. This includes government, municipal and corporate bonds. As will be seen, most of the stock exchanges have facilities for bond trading but the vast majority are traded over the telephone network. This is due to the fact that the majority of bond trading in America is conducted by institutional investors and can involve very large sums of money. It is presently more efficient to bring the brokers of both parties together directly than to utilise an exchange. In this respect, a similarity exists between normal bond trading and the execution of larger share blocks off the exchange floor.

BRITISH STOCK MARKET

The Stock Exchange in London is Britain's only equity market. In the nineteenth century, regional exchanges existed in the major industrial cities but their functions were finally absorbed by the London (technically, the United) Stock Exchange in the 1960s. Although London is the second largest exchange in the world, larger in capitalisation than the major European exchanges combined, it possesses several features which make it rather unique when compared to its major counterparts.

The Exchange is not Europe's oldest; this distinction belongs to the German and Dutch exchanges founded during the Renaissance in Northern Europe. However, it is the oldest in the English speaking world. In the late seventeenth century, it came into existence as the government and various trading enterprises began to raise capital through public offerings of stock. The government was integrally involved at an early stage in the development of the market and, due to the recent structure of interest rates and personal taxation in Britain, remains so today. The virtual monopoly established by the Exchange at that time continued well into the nineteenth century when many of the current trading and procedural techniques were introduced or refined.

One of the unique features of the Stock Exchange derives from Britain's international economic standing in the nineteenth and early twentieth centuries. It was, and still is, possible to trade shares listed in many other exchanges from London. This applies more to Commonwealth shares than it does to American ones but does, nevertheless, underscore the central role the Exchange can still play in international finance.

One important difference exists between the Stock Exchange and the NYSE which should be noted. When discussing the capitalisation of the NYSE only shares are included in the total figure. In London, the total figure represents both shares and loan stocks (bonds). If the fixed income debt securities are subtracted from the total, the actual capitalisation of shares alone is much smaller indeed. Table 1.7 shows a recent breakdown of the capitalisation of listed securities.

TABLE 1.7　UK Stock Exchange capitalisation　　(September　　1980)
(£ millions)

industry group	market value
fixed interest*	69 378
capital goods	29 715
consumer durables	16 332
consumer non-durables	29 374
other goods	107 606
financials	40 506
utilities	1 720
commodity groups	31 392
total	326 023

* bonds and preference stocks, all other
shares
SOURCE: London Stock Exchange, *Fact Book* 1980

The performance of shares on the Stock Exchange is measured by the Financial Times Index, an indicator broadly analogous in terms of popularity to the Dow Jones in that it is the most widely quoted (and it should be mentioned, the only major) single reflector of market activity. Gilt edged securities described below have their own performance indicator but the FT Index provides an adequate profile of share performance because of the homogeneity of the Exchange itself; no over-the-counter market exists outside the Exchange's influence. This factor affects new share issuance in that the Exchange will play a more central role in secondary type distributions than (for instance) its American counterparts.

TABLE 1.8   UK   Stock   Exchange
turnover   1964–1979
(£ millions)

year	total, all securities
1964	6 349
1965	20 486
1966	21 590
1967	35 956
1968	31 976
1969	30 390
1970	38 767
1971	64 192
1972	56 383
1973	55 769
1974	56 753
1975	94 036
1976	106 433
1977	173 333
1978	138 769
1979	168 936

SOURCE: London   Stock   Exchange,
Fact Book 1980

The Mechanics of Share Trading

The actual trading of equities in Britain is broadly similar to that in the United States with some obvious differences and variations, based partly upon tradition and partly upon the regulatory environment. However, the basic mechanics of shares themselves described earlier are the same.

The frequency with which shares are dealt, referred to as volume trades or simply volume in the United States, are called *bargains* in Britain. This does not necessarily imply that the deal was struck at a bargain but simply means that a trade has been consummated. One of the major differences between British and American reporting practices is that the former does not list the actual number of shares traded on a specific day. No mention is made of it in newspaper quotations. For instance, in Table 1.5, it can be seen that one notable difference with the American example is that the British listing makes no mention of volume at all. Otherwise, the procedure is almost similar with two exceptions; British listings include dividend cover and the pe ratio may be calculated somewhat differently from standard American practice.[10]

Customer orders do not necessarily specify a number of shares and the terms odd and even lots are not used. The volume for those shares actively traded is reported as the number of *marks* traded. An active share may have 25 marks in one day. This means that all orders for the day were aggregated into 25 different transactions. As with American procedures, the Exchange makes no distinction between a buy and sell order, or a short sale for that matter.[11]

The floor procedures of the Stock Exchange are conducted auction style and there is no real difference between its practices and floor broking procedures on the NYSE. Over the last two hundred years, a *single capacity system* has developed on the floor of the Exchange, quite similar to the specialist system employed in the United States. There are two types of brokers operating on the Exchange – *brokers* per se and *jobbers*. Brokers execute public orders on the Exchange but act through jobbers, the brokers' broker who makes the book and actually auctions the securities as a principal. The two functions are separate and distinct in the same way floor brokers and specialists are in America. This does differ substantially from the dual capacity system used on the continent where banks many times fill both functions for clients.

Margin trading does not currently exist in Britain although a form of trading does exist whereby traders may leverage themselves quite highly, albeit for a short period. Shares trade in what are called *account* periods, or in market patois, *dealt for the account*. What this means is simple: Stock Exchange account periods normally run for two weeks and an investor may deal in shares but not have to settle until ten days after the account has officially ended. In addition, if the investor wishes to extend this leveraged period further, he may arrange a *contango* with a broker. By this method, the shares are carried over into a new account period; that is, they are sold in the old account and purchased for the same price in the new. Interest, or contango, is paid on the money involved.[12]

Dealing of this nature can obviously affect the prices of shares, especially as an account period comes to a close. However, it is difficult to generalise about the effects of account dealing since the level of share prices will depend upon market conditions and expectation levels overall.

In recent years, the London Exchange has become more institutionalised as a process of intermediation, similar to that in the United States, has developed. The small, retail investor has been fading in the financial background in favour of institutional investors, aggregating his investment funds with those of many others. In evidence submitted to the Wilson Committee studying the structure and functions of British financial institutions, the Society of Investment Analysts attributed this institutionalism, and its effect upon share prices, to the increasing cash flows of the institutions given that the household sector had been a net seller of equities and had not subscribed to new issues to any significant extent. The reasons for this phenomenon are largely rooted in the nature of the British tax system and how it treats stock market gains *vis-à-vis* other forms of intermediated share (or other) investment.[13] These implications are mainly beyond the scope of this book but it should be noted that the Society of Investment Analysts and others maintain that if current tax disincentives against individuals holding shares should continue, intermediation will undoubtedly continue and institutional strength could reach some 70–75 per cent of Exchange turnover by the mid-1980s.

Institutional dominance has also led to an increase in large share orders being arranged off the Exchange floor. These block trades are known in Britain as *put throughs* and actually do form a sort of unofficial otc market in that they are arranged by brokers avoiding jobbers and the auction environment of the Exchange.

Despite the large number of individually listed shares traded on the Exchange, over 70 per cent of volume is currently dominated by trading in gilt-edged stocks (gilts); that is, Government issued or backed loan stocks. How this phenomenon originated and its actual and putative effects upon the financial system as a whole is important both for an understanding of the British economy and for the many parallels which are drawn with developments in other markets, notably the United States.

The Domination of Gilt-Edged Securities

Gilts are so named because they are loan stock (bonds) issued by the British Government and as such represent the highest credit quality in the country. Unlike the United States where the majority of bonds trade otc, gilts are listed and trade on the Stock Exchange because there is no otc market for them. (In 1980 a small 'unlisted' market was inaugurated by the Stock Exchange for small companies although, at the time of writing, it is somewhat early to determine whether or not it will develop into a large otc market). Over the last fifteen years gilts have become increasingly important both as investor favourites and instruments of monetary management. In the first instance, investors have turned to

TABLE 1.9   Gilts on the London Stock Exchange (March 1980)

	£ millions	%
Total market value, all securities	280 325	100
of which British Funds	57 765	21
Total turnover, all securities	168 936	100
of which British Funds	128 948	76

SOURCE: London Stock Exchange, *Fact Book* 1980

gilts for tax reasons as well as for the more prudential reason that they represent the best credit risk in the country. In the second instance, they have served as ideal instruments through which to mop up excess liquidity in the public hands by governments which have become increasingly monetarist minded.

Gilts will be mentioned again in Chapter 3 under their proper generic classification of bonds. However, as Table 1.9 shows, they have dominated the turnover on the Exchange in recent years, particularly in relation to their share of market value. Shares have also been quite popular in these terms but does this necessarily mean that Britain is undergoing an investment boom? Not exactly, because as both gilts and shares increase, albeit erratically, as proportions of the gross domestic product, one sector has virtually disappeared from the investment horizon – the corporate bond market (again, see Chapter 3).

The absence of a corporate bond market has given a great boost to gilts since the demand for high quality fixed income instruments is constantly on the increase by financial intermediaries. Gilt trading has also had a pronounced effect upon shares. As gilts increase their share of the market the more difficult it is for new or established companies to raise capital. Coupled with tax advantages over ordinary shares, the Government bond-cum-stock market has a distinct advantage over other financial instruments. There is a close analogy between the effect of extended leverage by American companies issuing bonds instead of shares upon the new issues market in the US, and the effects of the incursions made by the British Government in British stock market and its effect upon the capital raising process. However, the matter of an equity capital shortage in Britain is not one which can be adequately dealt with here.

Methods of New Share Issuance

The general methods of adding to outstanding shares were mentioned at the beginning of this chapter and they have somewhat immediate relevance to Britain because secondary distributions *per se* are rare if not non-existent due to the lack of an otc market. For a private company going public for the first time the most common method employed is an *offer for sale* whereby the company offers its shares to an issuing house which in turn offers them to the public. This method may be used to simply go public and replace private ownership with public ownership (no new money actually raised) or it may, in fact, raise additional capital. If a Stock Exchange listing is required a recognised broker must be called upon to aid in the listing process.

The secondary distribution in Britain does not follow American form. Normally, it takes the form of a rights issue, described earlier. The lack of an otc market makes the secondary distribution difficult because it deprives the new issue of an adequate market in which to trade and eventually become absorbed by an official listing.

These distribution techniques do not apply to gilts. New issues of Government stocks are offered to the public by the Government broker on behalf of the Treasury. This is normally done at the beginning of a specified subscription period. Initially, stock may be subscribed to on a partly paid basis, with the balance due at the end of the period. This has enabled many investors, dubbed *stags*, to purchase new offerings on a partly paid basis (perhaps 25 per cent of face value) and sell them before final payment is due, hoping for a highly leveraged profit.

New gilt issues can be allocated on a *tap* basis; that is, where the total amount of new monies to be raised can be acquired gradually rather than all at once. Instead of issuing £1 billion of new stock at one time, the Government broker will offer fractions of that amount in the market at periods conducive to subscription at that specified coupon level and maturity term. The tap then can be seen to be another tool of the various methods used in monetary management.

While their structure and functions vary slightly, the New York and London Stock Exchanges remain the two premier models upon which many of the world's other Exchanges have been based. This is true of many of the Commonwealth and Far Eastern bourses but is not valid in so far as the continental exchanges are concerned. In Europe, differences in the financial system compared to the anglophone societies have led to stock exchanges which play a more minor role in the national economies although the exchanges and the techniques of trading are, nevertheless, highly developed. The following sections will examine some of these markets in a general fashion to illustrate some of these differences.

THE CONTINENTAL STOCK MARKETS

The major European stock markets outside Britain are located principally in the member states of the European Economic Community and Switzerland. The oldest among them is the exchange at Hamburg, founded in 1538. The first exchange to actually trade shares in a public company was the Amsterdam Stock Market which traded the then novel shares of the Dutch East India Company in the seventeenth century. Prior to that time the various European exchanges, in their very rudimentary forms, were actually markets where any commodity or bill of exchange applicable to trade could be traded. When equities became popular they were traded as any other commodity until their continued use and proliferation necessitated stock exchanges *per se*.

Stock markets in Europe are usually referred to as bourses, named after the commodity exchange in Bruges, Belgium which was founded in 1360 in front of the home of the Chevalier van de Buerse. Second to London in terms of total capitalisation is the major French stock exchange, the Paris Bourse. In terms of volume turnover, Zurich is the second largest exchange. This somewhat paradoxical situation is due to the fact that while many companies are listed on the Paris exchange, only a handful are actually traded, while Zurich is an active centre for both shares and bonds.

Bank Domination of the Stock Markets

A phenomenon similar to that in London, quite different from the NYSE and American practice, is the high proportion of bonds among the listed securities on European exchanges. This fact tends to underscore the major difference between the Continental and anglophone markets and financial systems in general; the bond tradition is much stronger in Europe than it is in Britain or America. This is not to imply that bonds necessarily play any more significant a role in governmental or corporate policy, but does illustrate a major difference in both investor attitudes and banking practices. Generally, the

European investor has a preference for bonds over shares despite the long history shares have had in the development of many national economies. This preference has been created and nurtured by the role that commercial, all-service banks have played.

The specific reasons for the bond tradition are as diverse as the national economies themselves, but one or two generalisations can be made concerning it. As mentioned earlier, bonds are safer instruments than shares and this factor has provided an attraction to investors more accustomed to political instability than their British or American contemporaries. The psychological attitude has been aided by the large commercial banks in each country which dominate the financial sector of the economies. In most cases, the banks are clustered in small coteries of the most powerful which have survived the lack of political stability to maintain their hold on the respective economies. And in most cases, the banks have not been fettered by legislation restricting a commercial bank's incursions into the securities area, such as the Glass-Steagall Act in the United States.

An example of the banks' role in north European corporate finance can be found in Switzerland where new issues of securities, either shares or bonds, are invariably sponsored by one of the major banks which forms an underwriting syndicate with the other large institutions. These banks perform all of the chief functions associated with securities issuance, from underwriting and distribution to the actual investing on behalf of clients, both fiduciary and retail. In Germany, the main commercial banks, organised in the nineteenth century, also have a secure grip upon the secondary share markets. Only some 25 per cent of the members of the Frankfurt Stock Exchange are actually stockbrokers by profession; the rest are banks.

This German domination is not confined to the secondary market in terms of function alone; it also applies to its very structure. Of the thirty-odd equities having a major institutional following in Germany, the top three credit banks are consistently in the top ten active shares in Frankfurt, Germany's largest exchange trading some 50 per cent of the national volume. This provides the curious situation where the three largest financial institutions, representing 10 per cent of the institutional interest in shares, are traded by themselves and other banks on behalf of clients.

In the Netherlands, similar statistics prevail. The Amsterdam Exchange is primarily concerned with bonds and other fixed income securities. Again, both banks and brokers trade on the floor of the Exchange where over 2100 security issues are listed, over 1300 being

TABLE 1.10 New share issues as a percentage of gross domestic product

country	1972	1973	1974	1975	1976	1977
Austria	0.51	0.64	0.36	0.49	0.52	0.46
Belgium	1.77	1.54	1.32	1.21	1.08	na
Canada	0.68	0.53	0.52	0.78	0.69	1.33
Denmark	1.17	3.17	1.08	na	na	na
France	0.95	0.94	0.84	0.68	0.57	0.60
Germany	0.50	0.39	0.36	0.58	0.54	0.36
Italy	1.97	2.64	0.80	1.47	1.36	1.30
Japan	1.54	1.27	0.68	0.89	0.66	0.73
Netherlands	0.04	0.09	0.04	0.24	0.07	0.15
Norway	0.83	1.52	0.68	0.98	0.81	0.86
Sweden	0.47	0.35	0.68	0.95	1.25	0.59
Switzerland	2.69	2.24	2.25	1.92	2.25	1.87
United Kingdom	1.09	0.19	0.15	1.25	0.86	0.56
United States	1.12	0.86	0.45	0.71	0.65	0.61

na = not available

SOURCE: OECD, *Financial Statistics*, December 1979

bonds. And of the 800 shares listed, over 300 are those of American companies. This high number of foreign issues listed is also a predominant characteristic of the Swiss exchanges, which have one of the highest rates of new share issues of major industrial countries (see Table 1.10), due in no small part to the fact that many foreign companies actively seek a Swiss listing as a matter of prestige, public relations and vast investment possibilities through the large commercial banks.

In Belgium, of the 540-odd shares listed on the Brussels Bourse, about 33 per cent are of foreign companies. The new share market is dominated by rights issues of banks and public utilities. Banks are the usual underwriters of new issues. At the same time, the actual number of stockbroking firms declined in the 1970s as most institutional investors tend to have their portfolios managed by bankers. Germany provides similar statistics for foreign listings. Between 1948 and 1963 only 10 new listings were applied for on the exchanges. In 1965, 625 issues were in existence; by 1975 they had dwindled to only 470. But this did not dissuade foreign issuers. Over 150 foreign companies are listed in Frankfurt and over 50 per cent of them are American and Japanese.

Despite the fact that the Paris Bourse is the second largest share market in the EEC, most individual Frenchmen have assiduously avoided their share markets, favouring traditional and commodity (especially gold) linked bonds instead. It is estimated that less than seven per cent of Frenchmen allocate any of their savings for share investment. As a result, the country has the smallest number of shareholders per 1000 population of any major industrialised nation. The new issues market also reflects this (see Table 1.10).

Trading Techniques

Mechanics of share trading tend to be a form similar to the British account period. Basically two types of trading model exist. The first is a combination of cash and forward markets, used primarily in the francophone countries, while the second is the simple type of cash market used in countries within the Deutschmark zone. It should be noted here that the concept of cash and forward market as used for share trading in France, Switzerland and Belgium, is no different than the concept as used in the foreign exchange and commodity markets where the terminology is more widely understood and used.

In the cash market, called *marché au comptant*, all transactions settle the next business day. In the *marché au terme*, transactions are effective immediately but payment and delivery of securities may be accomplished in a later month, as specified by contract. Two types of forward trade exist, the *firm trade* and the *conditional trade*.

Under a firm trade, a buyer takes delivery at a specific price but has several options open to him: he may pay for the transaction at whatever date has been agreed with the seller, he may sell out the position in the interim, or he may carry the position over into the contango market, the *marché des reports*. In this latter sense, there is no real difference with the contango method used in London.

Using a conditional trade in the forward market, the investor has an additional choice. He may cancel out the position entirely but will pay a price, or *prime*, for doing so. This type of transaction is quite similar to an options trade, mentioned in Chapter 6.

CONCLUSION

Although stock markets play a similar structural role in most major economies even this brief discussion has shown that their functions can be quite varied. The major role that share trading has played in Britain and the United States has not been duplicated on the continent and the investor has played less of a role there in the raising of risk capital. However, a process of intermediation is occurring in both the United

States and Britain which, while not necessarily diminishing the role of shares in either economy, is nevertheless creating a situation whereby the anglophone and continental markets are moving closer together in actual function by allowing institutions to assume more and more of the risk process once shouldered to a greater extent by the individual.

NOTES

1. There is a difference between *authorised* and *issued* shares. A company takes the decision to authorise a new float of 1 million shares while only actually issuing 750 000. The balance sheet will take note of this discrepancy.

2. A market difference exists between British and American practice with reference to number of shares outstanding and the market price of a share. For instance, British stocks trade with lower per share prices than their American counterparts. But this is not to imply that their total capitalisations are different since British companies tend to have many more shares outstanding than do the Americans.

3. The traditional theory of the cost of capital holds that an increase in the debt structure of a company concomitantly requires an increased payout for shareholders. As the amount of outstanding debt increases, shareholders' equity becomes more risky since it is further subordinated to this new debt. The result is that shareholders demand higher compensation for their increased risk via higher dividends. A contrary view to this theory is found in the Modigliani–Miller theory which states that gearing (or leverage) has little impact upon the cost of capital to a company.
   See F. Modigiana and M. H. Miller, 'The Cost of Capital, Corporation Finance, and the Theory of Investment', *American Economic Review*, June 1958.

4. A common feature of ordinary shares is voting privileges attached to each share. For instance, if a company has 1 million shares outstanding and each common share has full voting rights then each share's vote is equal to 1/1 000 000. Preference shares may or may not be entitled to vote. They are referred to as voting, or the opposite, non-voting, preference shares, respectively.

5. Short selling can only be accomplished if securities are available for delivery. A short is considered a sale and thus securities must be delivered to the buyer in order to fulfil normal contractual

obligations. These securities are normally borrowed from other brokers or banks.

6. Commonly used fractions include $\frac{1}{8}$ ($12\frac{1}{2}$ cents), $\frac{1}{4}$ (25 cents), $\frac{3}{8}$ (37 cents), $\frac{1}{2}$ (50 cents), $\frac{5}{8}$ (62 cents), $\frac{3}{4}$ (75 cents) and $\frac{7}{8}$ (87 cents). In the over-the-counter market, and occasionally on the exchanges, $\frac{1}{16}$ or multiples thereof are used.

7. New York Stock Exchange, *Public Attitudes Toward Investing* (New York, 1978).

8. This is the opposite of the term 'disintermediation' which normally occurs during periods of interest rate uncertainty. Investors withdraw money from banks or savings and loan associations and invest directly in higher yielding instruments, thereby avoiding the banks and subsequently shrinking their deposit bases.

9. New York Stock Exchange, *Supply and Demand for Equity Capital* (New York, 1975).

10. The pe ratio is determined by dividing the amount of earnings available for distribution into the current market price (see p. 9). In the United States, this calculation is simple since profit after tax is considered the gross amount available for distribution. In Britain, however, the corporate tax rate is not standardised so pe ratios between the two stock markets may not necessarily be comparable.

11. Short interest is not reported in the United Kingdom.

12. Contangos form an integral part of theory surrounding future expectation levels of interest rates and commodity prices. This will be dealt with in Chapter 4.

13. See, for example, J. A. Kay and M. A. King, *The British Tax System* (Oxford University Press, 1978), especially Chapter 4.

SUGGESTED READING

H. D. Berman, *The Stock Exchange*, 6th ed. (London: Pitman, 1973).

W. J. Eiteman *et al.*, *The Stock Market*, 4th ed. (New York: McGraw-Hill, 1966).

J. C. Francis, *Investments: Analysis and Management*, 3rd ed. (New York: McGraw-Hill, 1980).

J. H. Lorie and M. T. Hamilton, *The Stock Market: Theories and Evidence* (Homewood: Richard D. Irwin, 1973).

Kiril Sokoloff, *The Paine Webber Guide to Stock and Bond Analysis* (New York: McGraw-Hill, 1979).

2 Money Markets

The second type of capital available to companies – debt – is divided into many classifications. It is also a major source of funds for those enterprises which do not possess equity in their capital structures; namely, governmental organisations at all levels from municipality to international organisation. In fact, debt is the most widely used method of raising capital and the capitalisation of the major money and bond markets exceeds that of the stock markets many times over. The major classifications are quite simple; it is broken down into short- and long-term instruments. Short-term debt is traded on the *money markets* while the long-term variety trades on the *bond markets*. The distinction between these two markets is quite marked but their functional differences are nevertheless quite subtle. Basically, money markets trade debt instruments with final maturities of one year or less while bond markets trade those with the longer maturities. However, this does not shed any light upon why the name 'money market' is used when discussing and trading debt instruments.

An illustration of how the market functions gives some insight into how it acquired its name. As a debt market, the money market loans a specific amount of money for a specific period to a borrower who promises to pay a specified rate of interest. When the obligation matures, the entire principal amount is repaid to the lender, plus the interest involved (unless the borrower defaults). The obligation itself in this respect is no different from a bank deposit or an IOU. However, what differentiates the type of instrument we are discussing from the simpler type of savings vehicles is also obvious from the name of this chapter. The nomenclature of market suggests that these instruments may also be bought and sold in a secondary market after the date of issue.

This is not to imply that the money markets only concern themselves with highly marketable instruments since a sizeable proportion of them are not readily marketable. As pricing mechanisms, these short-term bond markets value and set a rate of return, or yield, upon all instruments falling into their short but wide reaching ambit. Due to the shortness of these instruments' life span, there is one fundamental difference between short- and long-term debt. As will be shown in Chapter 3, a major risk of holding debt instruments is the length of time the bond takes to mature. The longer the holding period, the higher the risk to the investor and to the borrower itself, regardless of the nature of its business. But short-term instruments do not share this characteristic since, for the most part, in Britain and the United States, most money market debt matures in less than 270 days of issue. Thus, it may be said that debt with this short a life, possessing a secondary market, is a highly liquid form of investment comparable to actual cash itself since most of it may be sold upon demand. Hence, the term 'money market' for short-term bonds.

The major markets are primarily institutional in nature in so far as the average investor is concerned. This is due to the fact that the average money market instrument comes in large denominations only since the markets were tailored for corporate and governmental borrowers which have a huge appetite for short-term funds which can normally be supplied by institutions. This is not to imply that the markets do not affect the life of the individual since they are the immediate focus of reaction to governmental economic policies and the course of interest rates.

THE ECONOMIC FUNCTIONS OF THE MARKETS

As debt markets, the primary function of the money markets is to redistribute funds from those economic units in society possessing a surplus to those in deficit. Business and government enterprises, net spenders by nature of their commercial and social mandates, borrow from the household sector and other sectors which are traditionally net savers. However, this simple distinction will not adequately describe the re-allocation of funds in society because in practice many net spenders in temporary deficit may borrow from other net spenders temporarily in surplus. Equally, on the very next day after such a transaction takes place the opposite may occur and the lender may now become the borrower. The money market is the place where they come together.

Since most of these markets are institutional in nature, surplus households do not normally lend directly to deficit borrowers but do so through financial intermediaries. In fact, this is the actual process of intermediation described in a less formal sense in the last chapter. Intermediaries take the savings of households, aggregate them and redeploy them to borrowers meeting their institutional criteria. This becomes a form of intermediated investment with one substantial difference from the intermediation phenomenon in the stock markets: the intermediaries in the money markets are financial institutions and banks whose very business it is to perform this function. Converse of what occurs in the stock markets, at least in Britain and the United States, intermediation is a traditional function in the Anglo-American financial system while disintermediation is the anomaly.

Banks are the most predominant type of financial institution through which funds are passed by the saving public with building societies or savings and loan associations, life insurance companies and pension funds following in that general order in both the United States and Britain. Bank assets normally top their second competitor by at least 2 to 1 in both countries. This popularity provides an excellent opportunity by which to examine a bank's operations in the money markets as an example of fundamental techniques plus the general implications for economic policy.

Before discussing a bank's activities in the markets some very general comments need to be made about money market instruments themselves. It will become quickly apparent that there are two levels of money market instruments; the one which we have been discussing thus far (the instruments of corporate and governmental borrowers) and those which are essentially instruments of the professional market.[1] In this latter respect, one will also encounter interest rate levels (discount rate, federal funds rate, call money) which are not available to the average investor but which are set or controlled by central banks or monetary agencies. In all cases, the observations made necessarily tend to mix the two in market patois and at times it does appear that more than one instrument is being discussed. This is due to the fact that money markets are diverse and that several levels of short-term interest rates may come into play when discussing even one simple instrument.

Let us assume that a saver takes his money to a bank and places it on deposit. By doing so he is following the most common and safe form of investing his money. The bank will in turn take the deposit and book it as a liability and pay interest on it. In order to also enter the deposit as an asset it will have to find its own suitable investment. Normally, it will on-lend the funds to its own customer. However, it will not be able to loan out the total amount it received because of *reserve requirements*; those funds which it must retain rather than lend, as prescribed by local banking regulations. These reserves must remain in liquid form and are subject to daily change.

For simplicity's sake, we may assume that the reserve requirement today for the bank is $1 million. The bank finds that it only has $900,000 on hand and is $100,000 short of its requirement. The shortage is not necessarily reflective of the bank's overall financial condition but merely underscores the fact that operations and requirements change daily, if not hourly. Perhaps the bank took in a large deposit and simultaneously lent a similar amount and, as a result, finds itself momentarily short. In any event, it is in need of the money for one night only, until the reserves are again calculated the next day.

There are several avenues of recourse to obtain these funds. The bank could borrow funds overnight, go to the discount window of the central bank or borrow from a discount house. In most instances, it will borrow the money from a fellow bank or discount institution and this is what was meant by originally saying that institutions many times borrow from each other rather than from net savers directly.

The banks' activities in so far as credit creation and the credit chain are well known and will not be dealt with in any detail here.[2] However, if the bank took in a $100 deposit under a regime of 8 per cent reserve requirements, it would be free to lend $92. While the amount of credit created is crucial to the financial markets, especially in periods of high interest rates and inflationary expectations, we will centre here upon the $8 left as reserves for exactly what is done with it and how it is regulated directly affects and indeed utilises the money markets.

The amount of bank reserves in the financial system helps to determine the course of short-term interest rates. Any action which seeks to set higher reserves tends to make less money available for lending (thereby reducing the chain effect) and, *ceteris paribus*, puts upward pressure on rates until the desired effect is reached. When the demand for money is then temporarily abated, short-term rates should decline. Conversely, a reduction in reserves will have the opposite stimulant effect.

If a central bank desires to reduce the amount of credit obtainable by individuals or companies from banks it could obviously take other measures but manipulation of reserves, plus open market operations, are perhaps the two most widely used techniques in general. By an open market operation is meant the absorption or freeing of cash into the financial system at any point in time by the government. By selling treasury bills, the most common form of government money market instrument, to the investing public, a government can decrease the amount of liquid funds in the system while a purchase of bills in the market increases liquidity holdings (that is, cash) in the public's hands. These transactions can vary many times over the course of a week until monetary targets are temporarily reached.

There are obviously many more techniques that may be employed to siphon or add liquidity to the financial markets, control the current component of the money stock, and manoeuvre the course of interest rates. This brief description is only meant to illustrate how the money markets are utilised by both borrowers and lenders, as well as by government policy makers, to maintain an equilibrium (albeit imperfect at times, if not crude) between the supply and demand for money and its effect upon the workings of an economy overall.

Behind this maze of operations which occurs daily in money markets, one basic economic distinction tends to become lost quite easily. This fact will also be mentioned in Chapter 3 because it is true of all bonds as it is equities. This has to do with the difference between a primary and secondary market operation in the markets. As with equities, only a primary market operation actually raises money for a borrower. If the original investor decides not to hold the instrument until maturity and sells it in the secondary market, the borrower is no longer affected since it already has its money. Then the buying and selling of these instruments becomes a matter of importance only for the investors. And as mentioned earlier, the various interest rate, or financing, levels available to market participants are now of more immediate importance to those concerned with managing cash positions or directing monetary policy. However, borrowers continue to be influenced by these actions because they obviously help determine the future level of interest rates at which lenders will use the market.

SHORT-TERM INTEREST RATES

There are a variety of short-term interest rates in existence in any particular money market and it should never be assumed that there is only one rate for three or six month funds since there are, in fact, many. This phenomenon is attributable to two factors – first, the interest rate level for six month funds will vary depending upon the type of borrower and second, there is a difference between free market rates and manipulated, or controlled, rates although the latter are given direction by the market.

In the first instance, a government may borrow six month money through a sale of treasury bills while a large company does a similar borrowing through the corporate side of the market. It would be unreasonable to assume that both instruments will bear the same rate of interest due to the risk factor involved. The government instrument will bear a lower rate of return than the corporate paper simply because government paper is considered less vulnerable to default than corporate obligations. Thus, two various levels of borrowers operating in the market dictate different levels of interest to be paid. In all cases, the government rate paid for the particular period will be the lowest for that particular point on the maturity spectrum (see Table 2.1).

Similarly, there will be a difference in yield on three and six month obligations with the six month paper yielding slightly higher than the three month because it is twice as long in maturity. However, it would be incorrect to assume that it will be twice the yield of three month paper because there is not a multiple relationship between basic yield level and maturity date but only an incrementally increasing linear one under normal yield curve conditions. This will be more fully discussed in Chapter 3.

Market rates on treasury bills or comparable corporate paper are obviously susceptible to all of the actions of central banks or treasuries described above and many more. But one fact still remains concerning them: their yield levels are nevertheless determined by supply and demand in the market. The same cannot necessarily be said of other controlled short-term rates. The most common short-term rate which is directly controlled by government (i.e. central bank or treasury department) fiat is the *discount rate*. This is the rate by which central banks loan reserves to commercial institutions. Many times this rate lags behind market rates which often find new levels in advance of an official promulgation resetting the discount rate. This is particularly true in the United States where the discount rate has become known as a traditional laggard behind market rates.

TABLE 2.1   Yield spread: treasury bills *v.* commercial paper (3 months)

type	1977	1978	% 1979	1980 (May)
treasury bills	5.27	7.19	10.07	8.58
commercial paper	5.54	7.94	10.97	9.49
spread in favour of bills	0.27	0.75	0.90	0.91

SOURCE: Federal Reserve Bulletin

When discussing the relationship between short-, medium- and long-term interest rates the *yield curve* is normally referred to. This is illustrated in Chapter 3. As will be seen there, short-term interest rates are the lowest (normally speaking) of all rates because they are the shortest and have less risk attached to them in terms of time. But, due to the brevity of their lives, short-term instruments tend to most perfectly mirror changes in monetary policy or the demand for money generally and, therefore, are the most volatile of all rates on the maturity spectrum.

The term 'volatile' must be used in a qualified sense when one discusses bond prices and their fluctuations in response to changes in the course of money market rates. As will be seen in the next chapter, all issues of new bonds, whether they are long or short, are identified by the amount of coupon rate, or interest, they pay to the holder. However, when bonds are offered for sale in the secondary market they, as all commodities or goods, are stated in price terms. Any change in price will affect the coupon attached to them and thus change their yield. As a rule of thumb, for present purposes, the following should therefore be borne in mind: a 1 per cent fall in two bonds, one of very short maturity and the other of very long maturity, will result in a greater yield change for the short bond than for the long. But, despite the price/yield volatility of short-term instruments the risk involved in a 1% movement in price is still less than that associated with long bonds because at maturity date all bonds are redeemed at par, or 100 per cent of value and under volatile conditions it may take the long bond a longer time to recover its market price. Volatility in bond prices must then be understood in this context. The maturity term must therefore be understood in its appropriate price/volatility context.

DISCOUNT YIELD CALCULATIONS

Most money market instruments are sold on what is known as a discount basis; that is, they are sold at a price lower than par and pay back principal at redemption. Yield calculations on this basis are somewhat different than those for traditional bonds (see p. 69) since they are not stated in coupon terms but at a price which reflects the present yield levels in the market for instruments of a particular yield level, term to maturity, and quality. Discount yields are then a combination of price and yield conveniently stated together. When a

price is stated, the yield may be calculated through mental arithmetic rather than through more sophisticated calculations in some instances.

The example employed here will use a treasury bill of one year maturity in order to be as simple as possible. Assume that an investor purchases a one year bill returning 10%. The price he will pay will be about 90% of par, or in bond market terms, simply 90. When we say *about* 90 it is not a matter of imprecision but reflects that yield calculations can vary slightly between Britain and the United States. At redemption, 100% will be paid back. The annual rate of return is thus 10%. If, on the other hand, the investor bought a 6 month bill with a 10% indicated level, he will receive 5% for 6 months. Following this, a 3 month bill with a 10% level returns 2.5%.

Returning to this matter of seeming imprecision, it should be noted that money market as well as all bond yields are calculated differently in the British and American markets. Oddly enough, at first glance the discrepancy arises between the different practices of calculating how many days are in a financial year. In Britain, a year is considered to have 365 days while in the United States bonds are stated on a 360 day basis. The term 'one year bill' still means the same thing in both places but the 360 day basis means that an investor will in fact receive a slightly higher yield than on a 365 basis. Currently, the longest Treasury bill in Britain matures in 90 days so the following calculations are only illustrative of the difference in calculating UK and US yields.

Using the 10% bill, the 360 day method is calculated as follows

$$\text{principal} \times \text{interest} \times \frac{364}{360} = \text{discount}$$

then

$$\frac{\text{discount}}{100} = \text{interest } (\%)$$

or

$$\$100\,000 \times 0.10 \times \frac{364}{360} = 1\,011$$

$$\frac{1\,011}{100} = 10.11\%$$

The 364 numerator is arrived at as follows: a one year bill is actually 52 weeks multiplied by 7 days to equal 364. It can be seen that this method actually yields more than the indicated interest rate level.

The British practice follows the first two steps but operates on an actual day basis. The investor buying a full one year bill can calculate as follows

$$£10\,000 \times 0.10 \times \frac{365}{365} = 1\,000$$

$$\frac{1\,000}{100} = 10\%$$

If he purchases a bill which actually matures in 363 days to maturity his yield will fall below 10%. Equally, this procedure is followed for calculating bills purchased after issuance date. A bill with 8 months to run would be calculated as follows:

United States

$$\$10\,000 \times 0.10 \times \frac{240}{360} \times \frac{1}{100} = \frac{666.67}{100} = 6.67\%$$

Britain

$$£10\,000 \times 0.10 \times \frac{240}{365} \times \frac{1}{100} = \frac{657.53}{100} = 6.57\%$$

As mentioned earlier, the discount basis succinctly states price and yield in one convenient market price. In the example immediately above, the investor will pay principal or nominal amount (10 000) minus the appropriate rate of $667 or £657. Thus, the dollar value of this 10% treasury bill with 8 months left to maturity is $9333. The amount of interest can be ascertained at a glance by determining the discounted amount and dividing by the nominal amount, or

$$\frac{\$667}{10\,000} = 6.67\%$$

The same calculation is used for British instruments.

Discount yields are often stated in what is known as *coupon yield equivalent*. This calculation is used to compare returns on money market instruments to those on longer dated bonds which have coupons attached. In order to arrive at the equivalent, the discount yield must be converted into a bond yield, itself compounded over the life of the bond. American bonds normally pay interest twice per year and these semi-annual payments are re-invested (or compounded) in most bond *yield to maturity* calculations. Since money market instruments are simpler instruments, due to their short lives, the equivalent yield is primarily used for comparison purposes and does not figure into the selling price.[3] It is as follows:

$$\text{US equivalent yield} = \frac{365 \times \text{discount}}{360 - (\text{discount} \times \text{time})}$$

The bond equivalent yield is used for two purposes. First, if one were constructing a yield curve between 6 months and 30 years it would be consistent to use the same yield calculation for all bonds being plotted. Second, it is a necessary tool for comparing the yields on treasury bills with short bonds (those instruments in the short-term category because their remaining lives to maturity are quite short). If a bond with one year left to maturity was being considered as an investment along with a treasury bill the equivalent yield would be necessary because short bonds, regardless of maturity, are never quoted on a discount basis.

UNITED STATES INSTRUMENTS

American money market instruments are issued by the federal government, state and local governments, and corporate entities. Obligations of the federal government far outweigh those of the corporate sector, as Table 2.2 illustrates. The government instrument is

TABLE 2.2   US money market instruments outstanding ($ billions)

type	1977	1978	1979	1980 (April)
treasury bills	161.1	161.7	172.6	195.3
commercial paper	65.0	83.4	112.8	120.8
bankers acceptances	25.4	33.7	45.3	50.1

SOURCE: Federal Reserve Bulletin

the *treasury bill*, as it is in Britain as well. Treasury bills, or t-bills as they are more commonly known, are issued so that the central government can finance its short-term cash needs, and are auctioned at regular intervals. They normally come in a variety of term structures, with 3 months, 6 months and 1 year being the most common. When their respective yields (either basis) are plotted on a graph, they represent the short and lowest end of the yield spectrum. They are the lowest money market yields available because the government is considered the highest quality credit risk in the country. As will be explained later in this section and again in Chapter 3, debt instruments in the US are rated as to quality by independent rating agencies and those with a high rating bear lower coupons or discount yields than do lower rated paper. Put another way, if a corporation decided to issue a money instrument and there was no other comparable paper in the market by which to set a price level, it would have to price its obligation to yield more than a treasury bill in order to market it properly.

Since a large and ready secondary market exists for treasury bills, their prices will vary during their outstanding lives. For instance, assume that a bill was purchased at a 10% level for 6 months (the investor is receiving 5% for one half year). If interest rate conditions change, the price of the bill will also change to reflect this. If a new bill is issued two weeks later at $10\frac{1}{4}\%$, the old bill will slump in price to reflect this; a $9\frac{3}{4}\%$ new bill will cause the old bill to rise in price. Regardless of secondary market conditions, the bill will nevertheless be redeemed at full face value at maturity.

As mentioned above, the American calculation for discounted yields actually overstates the indicated yield level because of the practice of considering a year to have 360 rather than 365 days. However, in both the United States and British practice one other factor should be kept in mind when calculating bill yields in the context of total return to the investor. An investor with $10 000 to invest, purchasing a 10% t-bill for one year will only pay out $9 000. The other $1 000 is free for other forms of investment and can raise the total yield here beyond 10%. This method can, obviously, only be employed when the full principal amount is available for investment rather than the discounted amount only.

The Federal Reserve (Fed) utilises t-bills in its open market operations and can directly influence the rate of existing money market instruments as a result. When the Fed sells bills it is likely, *ceteris paribus*, that yields on existing bills will increase since the increase in supply suggests prices should fall. And if it buys up bills it is likely to raise prices and lower yields. Other factors may enter the picture offsetting this usual theoretical effect but this is the normal, expected outcome of open market operations.

A similar market effect can be found when new treasury fundings are such that anticipations of bill auctions can depress prices in the secondary market, thereby forcing the Treasury into higher rates than it might originally have hoped for. This phenomenon is no different than any other in the financial markets where an increase in supply is apt to depress prices generally. In the government's case, it is not its ability to repay the debt that is in doubt but the new funding itself. If the offer results in a large new net borrowing by the Treasury, suggesting that government borrowing on the whole is on the increase, the markets many times will read this as inflationary (suggesting an expanded budget deficit). However, a new bill auction and its effects upon the money markets should be distinguished from an open market operation conducted by the Fed in that this latter transaction is purely a secondary market technique designed to drain or add reserves.

The second most common money market instrument is the corporate equivalent of the t-bill, *commercial paper*. This instrument is actually an unsecured IOU of a corporation, issued on a discount basis, promising to pay the holder full face value at redemption. Commercial paper comes in a variety of maturity dates, closely paralleling t-bills, but normally does not extend beyond 270 days. There are approximately 900 American and foreign corporations issuing paper in the domestic market. Commercial paper of even the most highly rated US corporations will pay a premium over the comparable t-bill rate. This quality spread, or margin, can be seen in Table 2.1

In addition to American corporations, many foreign companies have borrowed in the commercial paper market. Normally, these borrowers must maintain a compensating balance and this is held in the eurodollar market by a commercial bank.

Commercial paper is rated as to quality by the two major rating agencies and their classifications can be found in Table 2.3. The rating a company receives for its short-term debt helps underscore the basic law of all financial markets; investors demand a higher rate of return on risky investments than they do on high quality, low risk instruments.

Other than the nature of the issuer itself, two features distinguish commercial paper from t-bills. First is the method by which commercial paper is issued. While bills are sold by treasury auction, commercial paper is distributed by two methods. One is known as *directly placed* commercial paper while the other is known as *dealer placed* paper. The

TABLE 2.3   US commercial paper ratings

Standard & Poor's	Moody's	description
A1	prime 1	highest grade
A2	prime 2	high grade
A3	prime 3	medium grade
B	none	lower medium
C	none	speculative
D	none	anticipated default

direct variety is sold direct to the public by the issuing corporations themselves while dealer placed paper is sold by a small coterie of well established speciality dealers, normally at a lower price (and higher yield) than directly placed issues since the largest and most frequent high quality borrowers are able to mount their own sales efforts while others must rely upon the dealer network.

The second distinguishing feature between bills and commercial paper is the differences in the secondary market capabilities of the commercial sector. The market is not well established and paper is often held to maturity by investors. The spotty market which does exist is usually confined to the paper of prime borrowers.

The two other most common forms of money market instruments are *banker's acceptances* and *certificates of deposit*. Both are traded in an active secondary market and normally come in large denominations. A banker's acceptance is akin to a cheque drawn on a bank by an importer or exporter with a future payment date stamped on it. Because of this future aspect, many holders choose to present it to the bank upon which it was drawn prior to the date. The bank will normally agree and stamp the draft as 'accepted' and discount the amount paid to the holder; the rate discounted will be above the t-bill rate for similarly dated paper. Bankers acceptances most commonly bear maturities of 100 days or less.

The act of accepting the cheque by a bank is a form of guarantee and the instruments become less risky than they would be without the stamp. And since they are used to finance import/export transactions their popularity and trading are virtually assured as international financial transactions continue. The return on these instruments can be seen in Table 2.4

Certificates of deposit are closely akin to time deposits left at banks by individual savers with one exception – true to their name, CDs are evidenced by an actual certificate and as such are a negotiable security. They have one great advantage over a time deposit and this lies in their

TABLE 2.4   Rates on banker's acceptances and CDs (3 months)

type	1977	1978	1979	1980 (May)
bankers acceptances	5.59	8.11	11.04	9.60
certificates of deposit	5.64	8.22	11.22	9.79

SOURCE: Federal Reserve Bulletin

marketable nature. Investors who place a time deposit and withdraw it prematurely suffer a penalty levelled at the amount of interest paid, as stipulated by Federal Reserve rules. CDs on the other hand, have a ready secondary market available so that if the holder desires an outlet he can sell it without penalty. Unlike other money market instruments, they have a stated amount of interest attached in coupon form and are not quoted on a discount basis. And one simple fact is sometimes forgotten when discussing them on an elementary basis. CDs are only issued by banks and financial institutions allowed to take deposits.

One other type of instrument deserves mention here although it is more common in the eurodollar bond market. This is called a *floating rate note*, or FRN, and is a bond whose interest rate is set periodically above a money market rate such as a t-bill at a specific margin. Normally, FRNs fix their coupon levels every six months. The feature that relates them to bonds is their final maturity; FRNs can extend up to fifteen years in length. The fact that they pay only marginally more than the money market at a floating rate certainly relates them to other instruments in this chapter. But the fact remains that floaters are still properly considered bonds because of the extended time risk involved.

BRITISH INSTRUMENTS

The British money market differs from the United States model not because it is in any way unusual or peculiar unto itself, but because the American banking system is unlike any other in the world. Unfortunately, many studies of monetary institutions and banking systems discuss the American type while relegating the British and other systems to secondary status or merely designating them as markets or central bank activities which are similar to the American practice. While it is certainly true that all central banks and money markets share some common denominators, these similar underpinnings do not necessarily imply that money market instruments are also similar.[4]

While American banks do use the discount window of the Federal Reserve, British commercial banks never deal directly with the Bank of England. Rather they employ a unique type of institution called a *discount house*, bankers' banks, standing between the Bank and the commercial banks. Discount houses perform a vital money market function by borrowing excess reserves from the commercial banks and re-deploying them into slightly less liquid instruments. These money market instruments are purchased by the discount house at a discount and either sold to another member of the banking system or held to maturity. The virtue of the system is that banks earn a market rate on their surplus reserves while the discounters earn a spread for assuming the risk intrinsic in a slightly less liquid instrument.

The Bank of England stands as a lender of last resort under this arrangement, lending to the discount houses should the commercial banks demand their reserves. The discount houses also become the practical conduits of the Bank of England monetary policies since changes in the *minimum lending rate*, the Bank's own rate for borrowed money, affect the discount houses by immediately changing the return on their own investments by affecting the discount rate on short-term securities.

Commercial banks in Britain also lend to each other through the *interbank market* for sterling, a market in itself similar to the trading of federal funds in America. But this similarity must be understood in context of one structural difference between the British and American systems. In the United States, bank reserves are stated in terms of cash; in Britain reserves may be held as cash, treasury bills and any other money market instrument which has a government backing of one sort or other. The composition of reserves can have far-reaching effects upon the banking system and monetary policy as a whole.

American banks holding a federal charter are required to be members of the Federal Reserve System but state chartered banks are not. Therefore, those state chartered institutions which withdraw from the system can avoid Federal Reserve policy, which is only statutory for its members under normal circumstances. The membership has been falling in recent years due to the fact that the Fed does not pay interest on reserves which it holds. If the particular commercial bank's deposit base is large this can mean quite a bit of lost interest per annum. In Britain, the problem is less pronounced since reserves can be held in money market instruments and the excess cash can be placed with the discount houses.

The nature of the discount houses and the structure of reserves is not the only distinction between the two money markets but it is nevertheless the fundamental one for present purposes. On the face of it, the instruments in the market are otherwise similar in function if not in name. But one similarity between the two is even more pronounced in Britain. The British market is almost entirely a wholesale market, not normally accessed by individual investors. There are several reasons for this which are alluded to in different ways in other chapters.

In the first instance, commercial banking practice in Britain obviates the need for the individual to seek out money market instruments directly. British deposit accounts are not regulated as to an interest rate ceiling as are American accounts regulated by Federal Reserve Regulation Q. Thus, British deposit account rates tend to parallel rises and falls in the Bank of England's minimum lending rate. American deposit accounts tend to be more stable because of regulation. Thus, under very high interest rate regimes there is less incentive for the British investor to disintermediate his funds directly into the money market.

The large wholesale size in which money market instruments trade is also a natural hindrance to the average saver or investor. Even though the average Briton has a higher per capita savings rate than his American counterpart and a lower per capita debt rate, the size in which these instruments trade is still prohibitive.

The major type of instruments are the treasury bill, local authority (municipalities) bills, commercial bills, and certificates of deposit and eurocurrency deposits as well as the inter-bank deposits mentioned briefly above. The oldest types are the treasury and commercial bills and short-dated gilts. These are referred to as the traditional instruments while the other instruments are referred to as the *parallel instruments* in that they have grown up alongside discount house operations.

Treasury bills play the same role in the British economy as they do in America although their popularity is somewhat less conspicuous as a proportion of gross domestic product than US t-bills. Unlike their American counterparts, British bills only have a maturity of 90 days and no longer-type issues exist. The vacuum left by bills is taken up by *short-dated gilts*, so named because they have five years or less to run, regardless of their date of issuance. In many bond markets, issues nearing maturity have a very thin market because investors normally are content to hold them to maturity or, conversely, avoid purchasing them, favouring money market instruments instead. But in the British case, short-dated gilts are actively traded and defy this general rule since the authorities have not issued longer dated money market instruments.

Commercial bills normally come in two varieties, *bank bills* and *trade bills.* These commercial debt instruments pass into the hands of the discount houses at some stage in their lives and are then sold back to a commercial bank and purchased by a discount house at a lower discounted rate.

Later in their lives they are sometimes sold to the deposit banks which then regard them as liquid assets. Trade bills are obligations of companies, again bought by the discount houses and then re-sold later to banks. In both cases, the process is similar with only the name of the bill being different. Bank bills are normally issued for 90 days as are trade bills.

TABLE 2.5   Yields on British money market instruments (1980)

type	July	Aug	Sept	Oct	Nov
T-bills	14.44	14.95	14.33	14.36	12.95
bank bills	14.84	15.87	15.00	15.94	13.36
trade bills	15.62	16.37	16.00	16.50	14.37
sterling CDs	15.30	16.62	15.68	16.62	14.37

SOURCE: Bank of England *Quarterly Bulletin*, December 1980

Local authority bills are also popular instruments with the discount houses. They are short-term obligations of the various municipalities and are often referred to as 'yearling' bonds. The market regards these as substitutes in many cases for treasury bills, especially when the latter become scarce in the marketplace, for whatever reason.

In the parallel markets, *certificates of deposit* are perhaps the most popular instrument denominated in sterling. They are issued for the same reason that a bank in Europe or the United States issues a dollar CD; in order to fund lending at a high margin. (This process is described in the next section.) An active secondary market exists for CDs, especially among the banks themselves. But when British banks desire assets in currencies other than sterling they are apt to borrow in the *eurocurrency market*, the centre of which is also located in London. This market is actually a pool of deposit funds held in London or other money centres of expatriate currencies, mainly dollars. When a bank has need of these currencies it may borrow (or lend) at a rate slightly higher than it would pay within the domestic economy of the currency itself. The virtue of this market is its easy accessibility to all its component currencies, especially those which may be protected by exchange controls in their home countries.

THE EURODOLLAR MARKET

Domestic money markets are utilised and controlled by institutions within a specific geopolitical area and have developed through both tradition and the peculiarities and demands of the financial systems they serve. For present, comparative purposes perhaps the most salient point that can be drawn about domestic money markets is that they are arenas where monetary policy is implemented. These general characteristics are not at all true of the one truly international money market – the eurodollar market.

After the second world war the US dollar became increasingly demanded in international transactions, supplanting sterling as the premier reserve currency. In the 1960s, the United States began to run large balance of payments deficits which meant that many dollars were being held in the hands of non-American citizens and corporations. This created a large pool of offshore dollars, ultimately nicknamed 'eurodollars'. This term denotes dollars held in banks outside the US, primarily in Europe and also in other offshore banking centres such as the Cayman Islands and Singapore.

Eurodollars are the largest portion of the eurocurrency market which includes, *inter alia*, Deutschmarks, sterling, French francs, Canadian dollars and Swiss francs. Many of these currencies became expatriated in the same way as the US dollar did, although dollars remain the largest portion of this market, estimated at 75–80 per cent of the total (see Table 2.6).

Eurodollars have their own money market rate quoted by the major banks in London (reference banks) holding and trading eurodollars. The rate is quoted on a term basis, in addition to overnight money. The usual term structures are 1, 3, 6, 9 and 12 months, and 3 and 5 years. Rates for these terms are quoted on a spread basis, called the inter-bank rate. A quote of $11-11\frac{1}{4}\%$ means that a bank will take a deposit at 11% and loan (to a prime customer) at $11\frac{1}{4}\%$. It is from the offer side of this

TABLE 2.6 Size of the eurocurrency market ($ billions)

	1976	1977	1978	1979	1980 (Mar)
gross	565	695	895	1155	1200
net	310	380	485	600	635
eurodollars as a % of gross	79	76	74	72	74

SOURCE: Morgan Guaranty Trust, *World Financial Markets*

spread that the eurodollar rate derives its name, LIBOR; the London Inter-Bank Offered Rate.[5]

The inter-bank rate is the one money market rate in United States dollars which can actually be described as a true market rate, not immediately susceptible to any domestic regulations or other wholesale rates. Unlike federal funds or the prime lending rate in the domestic American economy, it is not directly manipulated by either the Federal Reserve or commercial banks but allowed to find its own level through supply and demand.

The suppliers and borrowers of eurodollars are quite varied, coming from all sectors of the globe. The lending in dollars, in addition to the terms noted above, can be syndicated by international banks into longer term lending of 7–10 years in some cases. And many eurobond trading houses in London and the continent also use funds to finance their trading books and inventories in much the same way American traders utilise federal funds (see Chapter 3).

Besides time deposits, the major instrument in the market is the *certificate of deposit*. Time deposits themselves are not marketable but CDs certainly are, and also come in fixed and floating rate forms. Eurodollar CDs, as their domestic counterparts, are used by banks for obtaining loanable funds. As marketable securities, they offer a lower yield than deposits and, therefore, can be an attractive source of funds for loaning at or above LIBOR. For instance, if a bank were to lend a borrower money at $\frac{1}{2}$% above LIBOR (the size of the margin depends upon the credit risk involved) it could perhaps issue a fixed rate CD at $\frac{1}{2}$% below LIBOR. Its margin of profit is then a full 1 per cent, not the fraction implied by the bid-ask rate.

Until 1979, domestic American reserve requirements did not apply to eurodollar holdings of American banks but only to funds derived from the domestic banking system. If a domestic parent bank repatriated dollars back to the United States, the money was in some cases a cheaper source of funds than domestic funds, making them profitable for banks. But under the credit restrictions applied by the Federal Reserve Board in October of that year, domestic requirements were levelled at repatriated dollars. This was the first instance in the short history of the market where a domestic regulation was extended into the normally regulation-free atmosphere. This is in addition to Bank of England regulations imposing control over the activities of banks operating within the United Kingdom, whether they be parent banks or subsidiaries of overseas institutions.

The rapid pace of eurodollar growth and lending in the 1970s has prompted much discussion concerning the effect of this huge pool of offshore dollars upon the domestic economies directly affected by lending policies. The market has, at different times, been charged with promoting international inflation, creating havoc in the foreign exchange markets, and dangerously expanding the amount of international credit available.[6] In its defence, proponents of the system have pointed to the effectiveness of market participants in re-allocating funds between the industrialised and oil exporting countries (net suppliers) and the less developed countries (net brorowers). The market has been successful since many developing countries would have had greater difficulty borrowing without it. But, regardless of its virtues and drawbacks, little is actually known about its real effect in these particular areas, due in no small part to the fact that the international financial system has been in a state of constant flux over the last ten years.

NOTES

1. An example of a money market instrument which is actually a technique of the professional market is a repurchase agreement, or REPO. Through this process, an institution possessing a government treasury security may enter into an agreement with another to sell its securities at a pre-determined price and buy it back shortly, also at an agreed price. Normally, the purchase, or REPO, is at a fractionally higher rate than the sale, and is normally equivalent to the amount of interest the instrument currently yields in the marketplace. Thus, the seller temporarily receives cash and the buyer receives an interest equivalent. For a description of the various types of REPOs used in the United States see Marcia Stigum, *The Money Market: Myth, Reality and Practice* (Homewood, Illinois: Dow Jones Irwin, 1978).
2. The credit chain multiplier works as follows. The reserve requirement, as a per cent, becomes the denominator of a calculation dividing the deposited amount by the requirement. The result is the amount of credit created by the deposit. The $100 deposit with a 8% requirement would generate $1 250 of credit, or

$$\frac{\$100}{0.08} = \$1\,250$$

3. The equivalent yield used here is valid for instruments of 6 months and under. Equivalent yields on instruments of 6 months to 1 year are more intricate because of the longer maturity and the compounding effect caused by converting the money market instrument into a bond having two semi-annual interest payments.
4. A comparison of the British and American markets can be found in Andrew Crockett, *Money: Theory, Policy and Institutions*, 2nd ed. (London: Nelson, 1979).
5. Variations of LIBOR can be found in Hongkong and Singapore where inter-bank dollar rates are referred to as HIBOR and SIBOR.
6. For a thorough discussion of the euromarket, how it operates, and some of its problems see G. Dufey and I. Giddy, *The International Money Market* (Englewood Cliffs, N. J.: Prentice-Hall, 1978).

SUGGESTED READING

C. W. Clendenning, *The Eurodollar Market* (Oxford: Clarendon Press, 1970).

Andrew Crockett, *Money: Theory, Policy and Institutions*, 2nd ed. (London: Nelson, 1979).

G. Dufey and I. Giddy, *The International Money Market* (Englewood Cliffs, N. J.: Prentice-Hall, 1978).

George Kaufman, *Money, The Financial System and the Economy* (Chicago and London: Rand McNally, 1973).

George McKenzie, *The Economics of the Eurocurrency System* (London: Macmillan, 1976).

Jack Revell, *The British Financial System* (London: Macmillan, 1975).

E. R. Shaw, *The London Money Market*, 2nd ed. (London: Heinemann, 1978).

Marcia Stigum, *The Money Market: Myth, Reality and Practice* (Chicago: Dow Jones Irwin, 1978).

3 Bond Markets

In the first two chapters we have distinguished between equity and debt financing and the role that each plays in an issuer's financial strategy. This chapter will be devoted to long-term debt and the particular markets in which its various forms trade – the bond markets. Although short- and long-term debt instruments differ primarily by the length of their term structures, there are, nevertheless, fundamental differences between them. Therefore, it is not correct to assume that debt is debt, regardless of maturity dates because the markets treat these instruments in quite a different manner, depending upon sophisticated factors arising from that one basic difference.

In Chapter 1, the declining role of equity, both as a financing method and investment vehicle, was noted. As shares have declined in importance, bond financings have generally gained in popularity. This is perhaps truer in the United States and Britain than in some European economies for reasons which will become clearer later in this chapter. Presently, however, it is correct to say that bonds have assumed an increasing role in new financings in the major anglophone economies while shares have declined.

The New York Stock Exchange undertook a study to determine the role that equity financing would theoretically need to play in American corporate financing in the decade from 1975–1985.[1] The results have a twofold importance for present purposes. First, the conclusions reached illustrate that American industry is not raising the anticipated amount of capital required via new equity offerings. Of an estimated $250 billion assumed to be required over the ten year period, a shortfall of some $27 billion was already evident from the $25 billion annual average by year end 1978. Secondly, and perhaps most importantly, the vacuum left by shares has been filled by bonds. Table 3.1 illustrates the debt/equity ratio of non-financial American corporations over a twenty year period to 1975 (by debt/equity ratio is meant the amount of debt to equity

TABLE 3.1   Debt/equity ratios US manufacturing corporations 1955–1974

year	debt/equity ratio	year	debt/equity ratio
1955	0.209	1965	0.273
1956	0.232	1966	0.308
1957	0.246	1967	0.345
1958	0.244	1968	0.370
1959	0.239	1969	0.402
1960	0.245	1970	0.437
1961	0.250	1971	0.444
1962	0.251	1972	0.435
1963	0.253	1973	0.439
1964	0.254	1974*	0.469

* NYSE estimate.

Equity: Capital stock (net of treasury stock), capital surplus, minority interest, earned surplus and surplus reserves and reserves not reflected elsewhere.

Debt: (1)   Total short-term loans from banks,
(2)   Instalments due in one year or less on long-term debt, and
(3)   Long-term debt due in more than one year.

SOURCE: New York Stock Exchange, *Supply and Demand for Equity Capital*

employed in a company's financial structure). As can be seen from the table, the amount has grown dramatically over the period.

Why has this phenomenon occurred? Initially, it would appear that debt is cheaper in terms of the costs of financing than equity. While this may be true in some instances it is certainly not a statement which can be accepted across the board. For instance, a 10 year bond with an interest rate (coupon rate) of 9% can be cheaper, equal to, or more expensive than equity contingent upon conditions in the stock markets and credit markets. For instance, assume that a company wants to raise $50 million. In strong stock markets, when the shares are apt to be trading at a good premium, the dividend yield is apt to be low and a new equity issue might prove attractive, especially if the dividend rate stood at perhaps 6% of the current market value. However, in weaker stock markets, when the yield has risen to perhaps $7\frac{1}{2}$–8%, an equity undertaking would have to be compared to rates in the bond market. Thus, in many cases, the markets decide which form of financing will be used.

Debt has one general advantage over equity which again serves to underscore the basic differences between these two forms of financing.

Bond holders are creditors of the issuer, not owners. This means that creditors are senior to equity holders in the capital structure of the company; in the event that a financial crisis arises, bond holders must be paid before the equity holders are compensated. This holds true for the payment of interest and dividends as well as for the payment of principal. For certain types of investors, this safety can be of paramount importance. For the company, on the other hand, this also means that it will be able to raise the money it requires without adding new shareholders to the rolls. Bond holders are, for the most part, a silent majority whose interests are more muted and less politically and organisationally significant than the interests of the actual owners of a company.

For these simple reasons, and many more complex ones which are beyond the scope of this discussion, many companies have *leveraged* or *geared* themselves up over previous levels (that is, added debt at the expense of equity). But one significant factor mentioned in Chapter 1 should be reiterated here: this phenomenon would not have been possible unless investors provided the demand for bonds rather than shares. This investor element will be discussed again later in this chapter.

MATURITY CLASSIFICATION OF BONDS

As noted in the previous chapter, money market instruments normally mature within one year of issuance. Bonds, however, have maturities of up to forty years in the United States and in Britain a bond called a *consol* exists having no maturity date attached at all. Obviously, within this wide range some further distinction needs to be made within the realm of long-term debt alone.

Technically, a bond is a debt instrument with a maturity of longer than one year. However, bonds are rarely issued by corporations with maturities of less than five years. Governments and their agencies do issue instruments of less than five years and these instruments, albeit bonds in the technical sense, are more properly referred to as *notes*. Although there is no accepted standard usage in this matter, debt instruments with maturities falling within 2–5 years trade on different terms than do longer term instruments, and should be properly distinguished. However, one caveat here: *notes* refer to bonds issued with short maturities, not to long-term bonds with only several years left to maturity.

Bonds falling within the 5–8 year maturity range are referred to as medium-term instruments while those of 10 years or more are considered long-term. Terminology here depends to a great extent upon the market in which these instruments are issued and traded. For instance, a long-term instrument in the eurobond market (9–12 years) is considered 'intermediate' in both American and British market parlance. Term structure classifications will vary from market to market.

Bond issuers, whether they be corporations, governments or municipalities issue securities with different terms in order to finance specific needs. For instance, in order to finance an industrial project a company may structure the borrowing in bonds so that principal repayment does not occur until after the project has been assumed profitable; perhaps in ten or twelve years. A government may decide to borrow for twelve years because it has less debt to repay in that year forward than in fifteen years time. Or borrowing may be done simply to take advantage of what the borrower perceives to be favourable interest rates at the time. There are apt to be as many varying maturities on bond issues as there are issuers with different financing needs.

Each individual maturity category or term structure will have a different interest rate level attached. Ordinarily, money market instruments will pay the investor less interest than a five year note, which in turn will pay less than a fifteen year bond. The reasons for this are grounded both in investor expectations and the amount of risk associated with the debt instrument in question. Both of these topics are dealt with below.

THE TERM STRUCTURE OF INTEREST RATES

The amount of return a lender receives from a borrower can best be described as compensation for a risk incurred over time. The lender must have some indication of the credit worthiness of the borrower as well as gauge the amount of time his money will be lent; that is to say, how long it will be at risk. These two factors help determine the rate of interest the borrower will pay. Among borrowers of high credit standing, the amount of interest will, *ceteris paribus*, increase with each year outstanding on the bond.

Taken one step further, this simple concept can prove somewhat evasive if understood solely in terms of risk and time. Other elements such as opportunity costs enter the analysis and provide an element of investor expectations to the overall framework we are discussing.

Assume that a government decides to issue several new bond issues, or *tranches*, with varying life spans. One issue is to be for seven years while the others are for ten and twelve years. Each bond will be issued at a different coupon rate. Investors will expect to receive higher interest for the twelve year issue than for the ten or seven. But it may be legitimately asked what exactly is the risk in time if this particular government is highly regarded and not likely to default upon its obligations. Obviously, there is another factor yet missing in this discussion. If the investor purchases either of these bonds he may not incur any risk in terms of default but he does nevertheless incur a market risk; while he holds his government paper at $x\%$ interest rates may rise up to $y\%$ and he will be receiving less interest than the new prevalent rate.

How this rise in interest rates and its concomitant effect upon existing bond rates functions succinctly illustrates what is known as the *term structure of interest rates*. This discussion will assume that economic forces in an economy are functioning normally (i.e., no inflationary or recessionary pressures or tight monetary policy are present). Given such a condition, each bond maturity date will have a different interest rate level which will become higher as the term increases. This can be seen in Figure 3.1.[2] As it shows, the yields available on three year paper are significantly lower than those on issues of longer maturity.

Almost all graphs of yield curves indicate *secondary market* yields of bonds. These yields are those of bonds issued previously and trading

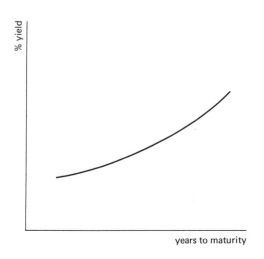

FIGURE 3.1 Positive yield curve

actively in the marketplace. These are distinct from new issues which have just entered the market for the first time.

These secondary market yields are used to price new issues of bonds. This is one of the major functions of bond markets. Assume for a moment that the yield curve in Figure 3.1 represents yields on United States government bonds and that the Treasury decides to float a new 10 year issue. By examining the yields on its outstanding paper it can gauge the price and yield level in order to fix the terms of the new issue. In some cases, the level may be lower than or higher than existing yields, depending upon credit market conditions and investor interest.

A normal, or positively sloped, yield curve is not the only type evidenced in the credit markets. There are many variations, depending upon the state of the market and the economy. Perhaps the most difficult condition is one represented by a negatively sloped graph; this is referred to as the *inverse yield curve* and is shown in Figure 3.2. This situation arises when short-term rates are actually higher than the long-term, reversing the normal order of events.

Inverse yield curves occur when short-term interest rate levels are raised to control growth in the domestic money supply. As money market rates rise, investors are provided with a disincentive to purchase long-term bonds since a higher yield can be obtained with much less risk by placing funds short-term. As more and more investors channel their funds into short-term instruments rates will eventually begin to fall off

FIGURE 3.2　Inverse yield curve

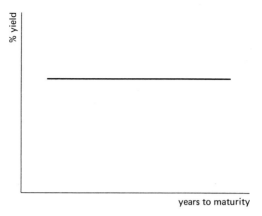

FIGURE 3.3   Flat yield curve

until the yield curve flattens out (see Figure 3.3). However, negative curves will not correct themselves through demand alone; the fundamental disorders which the monetary policy attempted to correct in the first instance must improve before investor confidence will correct the yield curve.

In the simplest sense, the term structure of interest rates can be plotted by taking bonds of the same or comparable borrowers and setting out their yield versus maturity structure. But in order to understand this concept in conjunction with how the bond markets themselves operate, several other factors concerning yield calculations and interest rate fluctuations in the markets must be taken into account.

THE CONCEPT OF YIELD

The yields employed in the bond markets vary in concept and calculation and one cannot speak of them in general without distinguishing among them. For example, a bond selling below par (par equals 100% of value) can have a different current yield, yield to maturity, and yield to average life. And these yields can vary significantly, depending upon the price of the bond.

A bond selling below par is said to stand at a *discount* while one selling above par stands at a *premium*. In terms of price, discounts and premiums are measured in *points* (1% of par value). In yield terms, they are measured in basis points, or $\frac{1}{100}$ of 1% (0.01%). Thus, a dollar bond which falls a point loses $10 in value, assuming that its par value is

$1000. A bond which falls 10 basis points has lost 0.10% points in yield; for example, from 7.5% to 7.4%.

The other significant factor to be kept in mind here is that the relationship between bond prices and yields is inverse. When prices rise, yields fall and vice versa. A bond which gains ten basis points in yield has dropped in price while one that loses ten basis points has gained. A yield gain is indicative of a weakening in price while a loss is indicative of a gain.

The simplest type of yield calculation employed is *current yield* (or *running yield*); that is, the coupon rate on a bond divided by its current market price.

$$\frac{\text{coupon rate (in money terms)}}{\text{market price}}$$

Bond prices are calculated as a percentage of par and then translated in money terms. This percentage is usually calculated on a bond of $1000 (or £1000) face, or nominal, value. Thus, a bond paying 9% per annum, selling at 98, has its current yield calculated in the following manner:

$$\frac{\$90}{\$980} = 9.18\%$$

Current yield is a limited and somewhat elliptical concept because it ignores the fundamental nature of bond risk – time. In this example, although we know the present yield, we have no idea of the true yield calculated over the actual life of the bond. If the bond had a remaining life of ten years, several additional factors would enter the picture.

At maturity, bonds are redeemed at par. The bond used in this example would be redeemed at $1000 in ten years time despite the fact that it is selling at $980 today. The capital gain of $20 (if the purchaser holds it to maturity) should be taken into the total return. Put another way, the investor has two returns due, one on the interest paid plus the capital gain. This can be expressed by the following formula, solving for r

$$p = \sum_{t=1}^{n} \frac{C_t}{(1 + r)^t} + \frac{1000}{(1 + r)^n}$$

where p = current market price
C_t = coupon payment at time t
n = number of years to final maturity

In everyday bond market terms, yield to maturity can be calculated by the following rule of thumb formula

$$\dfrac{\text{coupon} \pm \dfrac{\text{discount or premium}}{\text{years to maturity}}}{\dfrac{\text{market price} + \text{redemption price}}{2}}$$

Following the original example (assuming the bond was issued at par) the yield may be calculated as follows:

$$\frac{\$90 + \$(20/10)}{(\$980 + \$1000)/2} = 9.29\%$$

As can be seen, the difference between current yield and yield to maturity here is 0.11%, or 11 basis points. The only time that both current yield and yield to maturity would be the same is when the bond is selling at par, thereby eliminating the possibility of any capital gain (or loss).

This basis point differential will widen as the bond sinks to a deeper discount in the market; in other words, the yield to maturity will become greater than current yield. Conversely, if the bond rose to a price above par, the current yield would be greater since the investor would be faced with a capital loss at redemption; a bond bought at 105 will be redeemed at 100.

Yield to maturity is therefore the true yield on a bond, reflecting both current and future return. It should be noted that maturity yield must, at times, be adjusted for bonds whose average life is shorter than their stated redemption due to sinking fund retirements.[3]

Yield calculations must also be adjusted to recognise the frequency of interest payments to the investor. Bonds which pay interest twice per year (most United States issues and British gilts) yield more than bonds of a similar coupon paying interest only once per year (most eurobonds, regardless of the currency of denomination). This is an opportunity cost calculation but does nevertheless enter into investor behaviour.

In order to appreciate this concept, imagine an investor who has a choice between two US dollar bonds of a similar coupon rate. One pays interest semi-annually while the other pays annually. By choosing the semi-annual bond, the investor is free to invest his half year interest, thereby raising his annual return. The actual return itself for the year will depend upon the rate the investor obtains for his interest investment but it will, nevertheless, raise his total return for the year above the stated coupon on his bonds.

BOND ELASTICITIES AND THE COUPON EFFECT

Price and yield behaviour of bonds trading in the secondary market is, as mentioned earlier, the prime determinant in the pricing of new issues and the cost of borrowing throughout all segments of the credit markets. As with any financial instrument or commodity trading in the marketplace, bonds are affected by supply and demand factors but nevertheless do have their own peculiarities which, if misunderstood, can lead to an elliptical view of interest rate movements.

Assume that an investor purchased bonds of fifteen year maturity in 1977, with a coupon of 9%. During the next two years, short-term interest rates rose and subsequently new long-term bonds of similar maturity were issued with coupons of 10%. The secondary market price of the 9% issue would fall to a discount and if the investor attempted to sell it he would be faced with a capital loss.

But what would the market price of the 9% bonds be in light of the new yield levels? If all other factors are equal, it would be assumed that they would have a yield similar to the new issues. The investor seeking bonds at this particular point in time would be presented with two choices: either purchase the new issue with the higher coupon yield or purchase the existing issue with a similar yield to maturity.

This market condition can be seen in Figure 3.4 showing the demand elasticity of secondary market issues. As interest rates rise, bond prices will fall. But the fall will halt as secondary yields become comparable to new issue yields. However, demand will not become elastic until prices have fallen sufficiently to attract investors.

If these price falls are accompanied by adverse economic news (other than the rise in interest rates) some unitary elasticity or even inelasticity may set in for a short period. However, depressed prices on the secondary market will eventually encourage arbitrage so that yields will fall into line.

This is not to imply that all yields in the market will be congruent. Certain bonds will have higher prices than other comparable issues due to scarcity value and the structural nature of trading, plus commissions. Tax considerations also play a large part in determining yield, especially when demand comes from foreign investors. There is another factor,

FIGURE 3.4   Demand elasticity of bonds

however, which is partly financial in nature and partly psychological as well.

The above example compared a 9% bond with a 10% bond. Although these two coupons are certainly different they still fall within an acceptable range of comparability. But what happens when a 5% or 6% bond is compared with the new issue? The mechanics of demand elasticity no longer necessarily apply.

The *coupon effect* holds that bonds with low existing coupons will be more volatile in periods of interest rate volatility than those with higher coupons. The low coupon issue will plummet in price more rapidly than one with a higher coupon because the return to the investor becomes unrealistic as rates move higher (see table 3.2).

This effect is an example of the inelasticity of demand for such bonds; a price deterioration suggested by rising rates will engender little purchasing enthusiasm due to the fact that the low coupon issues are at the bottom of the range of investment choices outstanding. Implied in this concept is the notion that investors have a minimum threshold below which it becomes uneconomic to hold low yielding bonds.

Although elasticities are an excellent example of illustrating supply and demand within the markets, they do not always adequately describe the actual workings of bond markets since both the concepts and the trading arenas are imperfect. Thus, despite hypothetical examples used for descriptive purposes, it should be remembered that price levels are

TABLE 3.2   Bond coupon effect (annual yield)[1] %

	bond coupon			
price	*7%*	*9%*	*11%*	*13%*
100	7.00	9.00	11.00	13.00
98	7.29	9.32	11.34	13.37
96	7.59	9.64	11.70	13.76
94	7.89	9.98	12.06	14.16
92	8.20	10.32	12.44	14.57
90	8.53	10.67	12.83	14.99
% change in yield[2]	21.8	18.5	16.6	15.3

1. assuming 10 year maturities
2. due to price change from 100 to 90

determined by the availability or scarcity of the commodity involved. The assumption that instruments of similar character should trade at similar levels assumes perfect competition and/or perfect investor knowledge.

CLASSIFICATION OF BONDS

Investment in long-term debt instruments is part of the savings function in industrialised societies although the proportion bonds play will vary from economy to economy. Investors in different countries have varied attitudes towards bonds in general. One indicator of these varied attitudes can be found in Table 3.3 which illustrates bond issuance (all types of bonds) as a proportion of the gross domestic product of the major industrial nations. Although bond issuance will obviously increase as GDP increases in each country, it can be seen that certain European countries such as Germany, Belgium and Denmark favour bonds as investment vehicles more than investors in France or the Netherlands. The reasons for these preferences will become clearer when the individual markets are discussed later in this chapter.

Universally, bonds are classified according to the nature of the issuer. Generally speaking, the highest credits in an economy are obligations of the government. Other categories include corporate bonds, municipal bonds (local authority bonds in the UK) and, in some markets, instruments issued by supranational organisations such as the World

TABLE 3.3 Bonds issued as a percentage of gross domestic product

country	1972	1973	1974	1975	1976	1977
Austria	3.27	2.30	1.98	4.87	5.85	4.66
Belgium	11.12	9.00	7.72	9.26	8.30	13.23
Canada	2.87	2.26	2.70	3.49	3.41	4.86
Denmark	8.59	9.43	8.29	12.67	10.53	10.30
France	2.16	2.64	1.16	2.37	1.96	2.06
Germany	4.31	2.93	2.63	4.86	4.41	4.41
Italy	8.61	2.70	5.11	11.10	5.99	12.17
Netherlands	1.86	1.02	1.37	2.48	1.54	2.68
Norway	3.03	4.35	4.19	4.82	3.07	3.36
Sweden	6.47	8.16	7.02	7.98	6.58	5.57
Switzerland	6.69	6.59	4.59	11.27	14.70	8.97
United Kingdom	0.81	2.46	1.30	5.80	4.89	7.23
United States	3.58	3.18	4.19	7.02	7.69	6.96

SOURCE: OECD *Financial Statistics*

Bank and the European Economic Community. And wide variations do occur within these categories in terms of credit worthiness.

As the bond markets have become more international in scope, and especially since the establishment of the eurobond market in the mid 1960s, the credit worthiness of issuers and their debt has become crucial in determining which instruments bear the most serious investment consideration. The established agencies which rate bonds, as well as stocks, are the New York based Standard and Poor's Corporation and Moody's Investors Services. In Britain, similar services are performed by the Extel Group. In all cases, bonds are rated as to safety of principal and timeliness of interest payments.

Ratings provide the common denominator that modern portfolio theory requires in order to diversify both the risk and scope of bond investment. In order to determine the appropriate quality mix of bonds which will yield the highest return while, at the same time, remaining within legal or other parameters, portfolio and investment managers rely heavily upon bond ratings. Put another way, ratings help investors determine their indifference levels; that frontier on the yield curve they will not cross due to the risk of the bonds involved.

The ratings provided by Standard and Poor's and Moody's are set out in Table 3.4. Generally, only the first three categories of each are considered to be of high investment grade. This is true regardless of the category of bond.

TABLE 3.4   US bond ratings by service

Standard & Poor's	Moody's	classification
AAA	Aaa	highest quality, lowest risk
AA	Aa	high grade
A	A	high medium grade
BBB	Baa	medium grade, some speculative elements
BB	Ba	lower medium grade, speculative elements
B	B	speculative only

Secondary market yields on groups of bonds must always explicitly state the rating category of the bonds being used. This is especially important for comparison purposes and in economic analysis, since rating category yield differentials are often made in order to gauge investor reaction to economic events. During recessions, the yield gap between high and low quality American corporate bonds often widens, reflecting investor concern over those companies in the lower category whose businesses will most likely feel the brunt of an economic slowdown (see Figure 3.5). Comparative bond yields are quite important in financial market economics as indicators of economic trends and investor preferences.

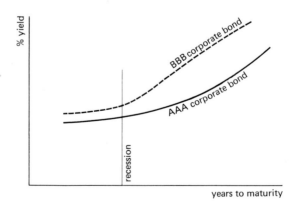

FIGURE 3.5   Quality yield gap, US bonds

THE FUNCTIONS OF A BOND MARKET

Secondary bond markets share a common trait with stock markets – they do not help raise new capital for issuers but rather confine themselves to trading existing issues. Their major function is to establish price levels so that supply and demand can find an equilibrium level, regardless of how short-lived that level may be. This function is distinct from the primary market.

The new issues, or primary, market is not an organised entity in most countries and does not have a central location. It is a term applied to the process of marketing a new issue, after the terms have been agreed. Normally, it is dominated by commercial or investment banks who manage issues. In the case of government issues, the official government broker has the responsibility of setting the terms of the issue and distributing it among banks, brokers and security dealers.

In most domestic economies, the new issues market is normally regulated by the appropriate central bank, treasury or monetary authority. Oddly enough, the United States is the major exception to the rule. The only restricting influences upon the bond markets in the United States are credit conditions themselves. Many European countries, notably Germany, the Netherlands, France and Belgium, operate what are known as *queueing systems* in their bond markets. Potential issuers are placed in a queue to the market according to their financial needs, credit worthiness, and political considerations. The regulatory authority is thus able to avoid congestion in the markets; that is, the markets remain relatively stable and the supply of new issues can be timed to take advantage of perceived demand.

Such systems are most effective in economies desirous of protecting their internal interest rate structures from the damage that can be caused by either a flood of new issues on the market or by the leakage of currency created by foreign borrowers. In the case of the United States, however, the sheer size of the economy plus the fact that the dollar is the primary international reserve currency makes a queueing system somewhat impractical. The bond market in the US has been restricted only once, in 1964, and then only to foreign issuers. More will be said concerning this under the United States and Eurobond sections later in this chapter.

An example of the actual bond trading process itself illustrates the economic functions of the secondary market and underscores the problem that can be faced when applying general theoretical ideas to the marketplace. Assume that an investor with bonds to sell approaches his broker (or bank in the Continental markets) and indicates his desire to liquidate the position. The broker will quote him what is commonly known as the *spread*, the bid-ask quotation on the bonds. If the spread is 95–95½ he may sell bonds at 95, or conversely, buy them at 95½. The ½ point differential represents the dealer's profit margin on the transaction; that is, assuming that prices remain the same while he completes both sides of the transaction.

This simple process is at the very heart of the pricing mechanism the markets perform. Naturally, this spread on the bonds is quite volatile and should not be considered as static; it may change from hour to hour. The one factor which does affect it is, *ceteris paribus*, interest rate movements.[4] And this risk also affects the major participants in the secondary market as well as investors. Bond dealers finance their own inventories of bonds in much the same way that margin traders do in the stock markets (refer to Chapter 1); that is, by borrowing money. The cost of these funds can have a major impact upon price levels in the secondary market.

A dealer normally buys bonds for his own account utilising overnight or other short-term funds in the same manner that money market traders do. A dealer taking a position in 9% bonds worth $1 million would borrow the money (under normal interest rate conditions) at perhaps 7½%. Thus, he may keep the bonds in his inventory until they are placed with a final purchaser since the cost of funding is less than the interest he will receive on the principal amount. This is shown in Figure 3.6.

Under inverse yield curve conditions the borrowed money will cost

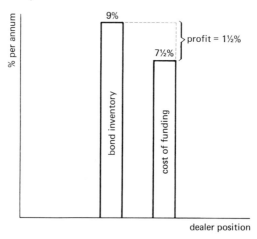

FIGURE 3.6   Dealer bond funding

more than the bond interest rate so the dealer is losing money while he seeks to place the bonds with reluctant buyers. When this condition occurs – when a large quantity of bonds, and especially new issues, is held by dealers rather than final investors – it is commonly referred to as *overhang*, that point where supply exceeds demand.

Any situation of this nature indicates disequilibrium in the marketplace. In the case of bond markets, it does have one additional effect. When many dealers are faced with such a condition they will eventually be forced to sell off their inventories in order to reduce their liability rather than hold on for improved conditions. As they do so, prices become depressed. This is what is referred to as *professional selling*. Whether or not demand becomes elastic or inelastic thereafter will depend to a great extent upon how resources are allocated among dealers themselves plus the interest rate conditions which originally created the inverse yield curve situation.

These elementary market functions will naturally vary from market to market. Each of the major individual markets will be discussed further as well as the nature of the investors who purchase bonds.

BOND INVESTORS

In the previous chapters, we have seen that each financial market attracts a special type of investor who utilises it for very specific reasons. The same is true of the bond markets but one particular question does arise which is unique to the long-term nature of this market – why would an investor buy an instrument yielding perhaps 9%, maturing in 15 years when he might do equally well or better in shorter-term instruments of one nature or other?

A term normally applied to commodity or foreign exchange markets also applies to bond markets and adequately describes this particular time phenomenon – *hedging*. This is the process whereby assets are matched against liabilities of similar nature (and for a similar period of time) in order to eliminate risk.

In the majority of cases, bonds are purchased by institutions or individuals who have a specific reason for locking into a yield for a long period of time. The institutions normally include insurance companies, pension funds, unit trusts and others involved in fiduciary activities, all of whom require a guaranteed annual return on their investments. An insurance company may determine that it needs a 9% annual return in order to offset actuarially projected payments on claims. By purchasing a quality bond of that coupon level it insures that these projections will be met. The same is true of a pension fund, entrusted with retirement monies. It must invest in long-term instruments guaranteeing a rate of return in order to protect the employees contributing to it.

This is not to imply that bonds are not purchased by individuals since they do represent a viable high yielding conduit for personal savings. But the overall demand for bonds and the role they play in the savings and investment functions vary from country to country. The individual markets are the best microcosm of this.

BOND MARKETS – DOMESTIC AND INTERNATIONAL

United States

In the United States markets, there are three types of bond issuers – the United States government and its various agencies, corporations, and state and local governments (generically referred to as *municipal* issues). Between them, they comprise the world's largest single debt market although they are rarely referred to as a single entity. And each compartment alone is the largest of its kind in the world (see Table 3.5).

The rate of interest paid on these various instruments varies according to the issuer. Coupon rates on municipal bonds are lower than those of the other two varieties. This situation has been created because interest paid on municipal issues is exempt from federal income tax. This exemption stems from an early nineteenth-century Supreme Court ruling which held that the federal government did not have the power to tax the states and, concomitantly, municipal entities within the states. Therefore, municipal bond interest is free from federal tax. Conversely interest on federal government obligations is free from individual state taxation.

TABLE 3.5   Domestic bond issues in the US ($ millions)

type	1977	1978	1979	1980 (Feb)
state and local government	46 769	48 607	43 490	5 363
corporate	42 015	36 872	36 690	6 915
US government*	47 000	60 000	74 700	76 400

* amount of total bonds outstanding, excludes bills and notes.

SOURCE: Federal Reserve Bulletin

As a result, coupon rates on municipal paper can be as much as 200 basis points (2%) lower than on similarly rated corporate paper. Municipal issues have their own interest rate structure but are, nevertheless, affected by general interest rate movements in the capital markets.

Among the other two categories, the rates on United States government paper are lower than those on corporate paper, reflecting the high credit rating assigned to government issues. For this safety, the investor gives up yield when he invests in such bonds.

The yields on corporate bonds are the highest of these groups although substantial discrepancies exist within this general category. The yields on the highest grade corporate and municipal issues versus those of the federal government are shown in Figure 3.7.

Throughout this discussion, we have referred only to bonds known in bond market patois as *straights*; issues with a specific coupon rate due on a specified future date. Within the United States, as in a great many other markets, many other variations exist. *Convertible bonds* are debt obligations normally convertible into a specified number of ordinary shares of the issuing corporation. *Floating rate notes* are bonds issued for a specified time period but the interest rate varies. Normally, it is fixed at 3 or 6 monthly intervals above a money market rate; usually the treasury bill rate prevalent at the time.

Due to the size of the New York Stock Exchange, convertible bonds are popular instruments since they offer a fixed rate of interest (although normally lower than that on straight bonds) plus the potential for capital appreciation via the shares. Floating rate notes are especially popular in times of interest rate uncertainty since, being pegged to money market rates, they are the only bonds which can overcome the vagaries and lost opportunity costs inflicted by inverse yield curves.

Government securities trade over-the-counter in the United States as do municipal issues. Corporate issues may be traded on the NYSE (if they are listed) but most orders are, in fact, filled over-the-counter. Despite this seemingly diverse market, the reporting procedures for dealings done established by the various regulatory authorities has created a standard and relatively efficient market within each compartment.

Foreign bonds
A separate category of bonds exists within the US referred to as foreign or *Yankee* bonds. These instruments are issued by foreign governments, corporations and some municipalities and are denominated in United

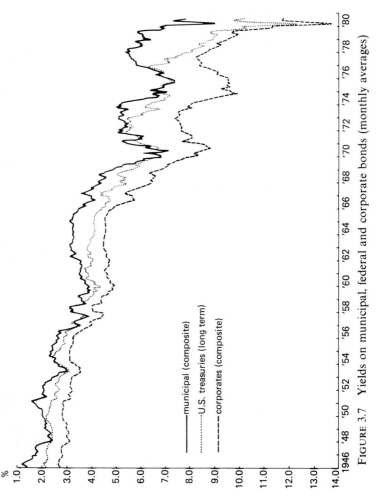

FIGURE 3.7 Yields on municipal, federal and corporate bonds (monthly averages)

SOURCE: Moody's Investor Services

States dollars. These bonds pay interest and trade in normal United States fashion.[5] In almost all cases, they are highly rated instruments and are comparable in the eyes of the market to high rated United States corporations.

Yankee bonds are floated by borrowers desirous of United States dollars, for whatever reason. Traditionally, they yield more than comparable United States issues due to their foreign nature. A yield differential must therefore be attached in order to market these instruments effectively. At year end 1978, the Yankee bond market was capitalised at about $20 billion nominal value.

The foreign sector of the American market was the only compartment of the American market ever subject to any sort of capital controls. In the mid 1960s, the US suffered a balance of payments disequilibrium caused in part by a large net outflow of long-term investment funds. In order to redress part of this problem, limitations were placed upon domestic investors purchasing foreign securities. This was accomplished through the Interest Equalisation Tax of 1964 (IET). Effectively, this measure closed the American capital market to foreign borrowers for ten years by taxing the yield premium foreign securities paid over their comparable American counterparts. The market again became active in 1974–75 when the IET was lifted but the yield premium on these foreign securities again re-emerged for many of the same reasons. Issuing activity in Yankee bonds can be found in Table 3.6.

TABLE 3.6   Yankee bond issues ($ millions)

	1977	1978	1979	1980
total	7 428	5 795	4 515	1 729
of which				
Canadian entities	3 022	3 142	2 193	870
international organs	1 917	459	1 100	350
other	2 489	2 194	1 222	509

SOURCE: Morgan Guaranty Trust, *World Financial Markets*

United Kingdom

At present, the bond market in the United Kingdom is limited to two sectors, British government debt issues (gilts) and local authority (analogous to United States municipal) issues. The market for corporate issues has not existed for over a decade. This situation has arisen because of the high inflation rates Britain has suffered in recent years. As inflation moved into double figures, the cost of corporate borrowing soared, making bond borrowing impractical. As a result, many corporate borrowers turned to their traditional source of funds, the clearing banks, for medium- and long-term funds.

Government bond trading is not accomplished in the same manner as in the United States. Although gilts take the form of straight bonds, with a fixed coupon and redemption date, these instruments trade primarily on the London Stock Exchange in the same way shares do. Interest is paid semi-annually and at interest payment date, the stocks trade *ex interest* (similar to *ex dividend* for shares).

Because gilts trade on the Exchange, as well as London's reputation as an international financial centre, the instruments have attracted a great deal of international investment interest. Coupled with the domestic demand from pension funds and other institutional investors this has made traditionally high yielding (Figure 3.8) gilts perhaps the best known of all British investment vehicles. The increasing need for debt financing by the British Treasury currently continues to dominate the domestic bond market as such, in many cases to the continuing detriment of domestic corporate borrowers.

Unlike in many open economies, British based investors were not able to freely purchase foreign securities because sterling was protected by exchange controls. In the case of security investment, the *investment premium* added a premium to the purchase of foreign securities, only

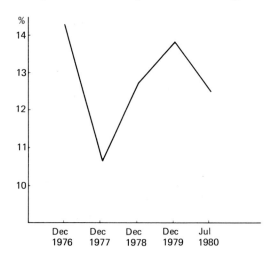

FIGURE 3.8   Long-term UK gilt yield

adding to their expense. Gilts then become the only viable fixed income alternative to investors as long as exchange controls remained in place.

The British authorities operate what is known as a *tap stock* system whereby the amount of gilts offered on a new issue may be regulated by the government broker. A new issue of gilts may be offered in bits to the investing public so that the authorities have some control over demand. If demand is poor, the tap may be turned off temporarily and vice versa. Also, through such a method, the authorities are able to maintain some control over secondary market yields.

Although gilt yields have, in recent years, been below the UK inflation rate, the negative net return has not dissuaded domestic investors due to the lack of suitable high yielding alternatives. This is also true of non-sterling based investors. If gilt returns are high enough to attract foreign interest and the future of sterling itself is optimistic, foreign investors will convert their cash into pounds in order to purchase gilts. As long as the currency does not depreciate during the investor's holding period, the gilt yield, although low in UK inflation terms, may still be better than the overall return in the investor's home country.

Local authority bonds are the second most popular form of long-term debt in Britain. They are divided into two types – *yearling* bonds normally have maturities of one year and the longer term variety have maturities in excess of five years. Coupon rates depend upon the quality of the municipality issuing the paper plus the term involved.

Because of the difficulties with inflation rates in Britain, banks have come to assume an increasing role in corporate finance. Corporate borrowers have eschewed bond financings in favour of overdrafts with their bank. Although this form of financing is normally for the short-term, by rolling over the principal on due date the banks have aided industry in its need for capital on a long-term basis. But neither this process nor the absence of the corporate market itself has prevented some British companies from borrowing in the eurobond market; a phenomenon we shall discuss in that particular section below.

The Continental Markets

Bond financings and investment have traditionally played a larger role in the major European countries than elsewhere for several reasons. The high savings ratios of European investors has meant that a high proportion of their incomes has been lodged with their commercial banks. These institutions in turn invest funds on behalf of their clients in bonds and also act as investment bankers for a large proportion of native industry. The result has been that banks have performed a twofold function: they both invest savings and raise capital, serving as efficient conduits of funds to industry.

This function has a long history on the continent. The banks have played a pivotal role in many economies for over one hundred years and have weathered numerous wars and political upheavals. They have proved much more resilient than the European stock markets in this respect and, as a result, share investment has normally taken a back seat to bond investment. Added to this is the fact that commercial banks are also able to perform investment banking functions (underwriting) unlike their American counterparts who are restricted under the Glass-Steagall Act. These combined functions have created a different sort of investment behaviour from that which exists in the United States and, to a lesser extent, in Britain.

After the second world war, many European economies were protected by exchange controls in order to aid their recoveries. Since then, many of the controls have been lifted and today the bond markets in Holland, Switzerland and Germany enjoy international investor interest. Foreign bonds issued in these countries are shown in Table 3.7. This issuing activity is in large part due to the fact that these currencies have proved strong on the foreign exchange markets.

Bond trading on the continent centres around the various stock exchanges, where many of the bonds are listed. This is not to imply that over-the-counter trading does not occur but the exchanges do play a more central role here.

A good deal of currency switching and bond investing between European currencies exists on the same basic lines that were outlined in the section above on British gilts. This cross border investing is facilitated by the foreign exchange activities provided by the major banks, many of which operate sophisticated forward markets in the major currencies. Thus, when interest rate differentials between continental bond markets occur (Figure 3.9) a certain amount of

TABLE 3.7   Foreign bond issues in Europe ($ billions equivalent)

country	1977	1978	1979	1980 (Aug)
Germany	2.18	3.78	5.38	2.61
Switzerland	4.97	5.70	9.78	7.53
Netherlands	0.21	0.38	0.07	na

SOURCE: Morgan Guaranty Trust, *World Financial Markets*

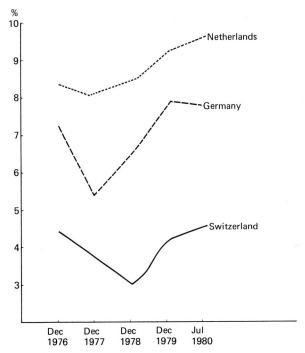

FIGURE 3.9   Long-term European government bond yields

currency switching will also occur and some narrowing of these differentials may take place.

The major types of bonds described in the previous sections also exist in Europe but other variations also exist which have never become popular in the United States or Britain. For instance, in France several types of bonds exist which are indexed to the price of gold or other commodities. Finland at one time experimented with public bonds indexed to the inflation rate. All of these varieties only accentuate a strong bond tradition; without it such variations would never have been possible.

In some countries, notably Holland and Belgium, debt instruments assume slightly different forms than the bonds we have examined previously. Many times they are referred to as debt certificates and their issuance and secondary market trading depend upon the commercial banks. These instruments can at times form a large part of overall bond issues in any given year.

The Eurobond Market

During the late 1950s and early 1960s the United States dollar supplanted sterling as the primary reserve currency used in international financial transactions. Since the United States was free of capital and exchange controls, a large amount of dollars found their way into European and other offshore banks where they were held as dollars rather than being converted into another currency. These expatriate dollars were not subject to Federal Reserve requirements so the *eurodollar* market became an important and easily accessible source of funds.

In the mid-1960s, the United States imposed capital controls upon both domestic and foreign borrowers. Domestic borrowers were not permitted to export domestic funds and foreign borrowers (with some exceptions) were denied access to the United States capital market by the IET. As a result, many borrowers needing dollars turned instead to the eurodollar market and a eurodollar bond market was born.

Eurobonds, whether they be dollar instruments or denominated in another eurocurrency, are bonds issued by a borrower outside its country of residence and syndicated by an international group of banks. They are usually listed on the stock exchanges in London, Luxembourg, or sometimes Holland. Normally, they pay a slight coupon premium over a comparable bond issued in a domestic market due to their expatriate nature.

These bonds are denominated in other currencies as well. The Deutschmark is the second most popular currency of denomination although some control is exercised over their issuance by the German capital markets authorities. Other popular currencies of denomination include the Canadian dollar, French franc, Dutch guilder, Norwegian kroner, Kuwaiti dinar and some artificial currency units such as the European Unit of Account and Special Drawing Right. Issuing activity in these various currencies can be found in Table 3.8.

Due to their international nature, eurobonds trade over-the-counter in the major financial centres of Europe, Asia and North America. Although the market is capitalised at over $100 billion equivalent, making it the second largest bond market in the world behind the United States, secondary market trading can be erratic because of this international scope. Therefore, the elasticities described earlier in this chapter are more difficult to apply in some instances.

As an external marketplace, the eurobond market is able to raise funds for borrowers limited either by size of their own domestic markets

TABLE 3.8   Currencies of eurobond denomination ($ millions or equivalent)

currency	1977	1978	1979	1980 (Aug)
US dollar	11 627	7 290	12 565	10 794
Deutschmark	4 131	5 251	3 626	2 582
Dutch guilder	452	394	531	750
Canadian dollar	655	0	425	214
European Unit of Account	28	165	253	25
others	878	1 025	1 326	1 510

SOURCE: Morgan Guaranty Trust, *World Financial Markets*

or by capital controls. It was able to provide funds for a great many United States corporations limited by United States controls and still provides funds (under certain domestic conditions) to British borrowers and others whose domestic markets are dominated by government or bank issuers.

This same internationalism also adds one additional element of risk in this sector not evidenced in purely domestic bond markets – currency risk. The prices of bonds in the euromarket are highly susceptible to currency fluctuations and this factor, along with the ever present interest rate risk, can make the market highly volatile in times of economic uncertainty.

NOTES

1. *The Demand and Supply for Equity Capital* (New York, 1975).
2. When comparing the term structure of interest rates, it should be noted that the classification of bonds used is all important. For instance, the term structures (yield curves) on government issued bonds will be in a low yielding curve when compared to corporate issuers although the shape of the curve will be the same.
3. Sinking fund redemptions reduce the stated life of a bond. For instance, a bond issued for a fifteen year period may have mandatory sinking fund redemptions attached which set aside bonds for retirement after the fourth year. Thus, the bond may have a life of only 11 or 12 years rather than the original fifteen. Yield to maturity (in these cases, *yield to average life*) must take account of the shortened lifespan.
4. In the eurobond market and foreign bond markets currency considerations also play a major role in investment risk.

5. Bonds issued by United States borrowers pay interest twice per year. Yankee bonds follow this practice although the issuer may be acquainted with other practices. United States bonds also normally trade with interest attached. This is known as accrued interest. If a buyer purchases bonds a month after an interest payment date he must pay the seller the interest and this is added to the purchase price. This practice is followed in most countries except the United Kingdom where gilts trade *ex interest* (*ex dividend* fashion) following stock market practice.

SUGGESTED READING

David Darst, *The Complete Bond Book* (New York: McGraw-Hill, 1975).

J. C. Dodds and J. L. Ford, *The Term Structure of Interest Rates* (London: Martin Robertson, 1974).

Paul Einzig, *The Eurobond Market* (London: Macmillan, 1970).

Charles R. Geisst, *Raising International Capital: International Bond Markets and the European Institutions* (Farnborough: Saxon House, 1980).

Sidney Homer and M. Liebowitz, *Inside the Yield Book* (New York: Prentice-Hall, 1972).

Sidney Homer, *A History of Interest Rates* (New Brunswick: Rutgers University Press, 1963).

James Van Horne, *Financial Market Rates and Flows* (Englewood Cliffs, N.J.: Prentice-Hall, 1978).

4 Commodity Futures Markets

Commodity markets differ from equity or bond markets in one fundamental respect. The instruments traded on their floors are not present assets but future contracts calling for delivery of an asset. For this reason, they are universally referred to as futures markets. Trading in the future is a process originating with farmers several hundred years ago yet, at first encounter, these markets are perhaps the most difficult of all financial markets to understand.

Futures markets also have the most exotic reputation of all the financial markets. The general public seems to know them, if at all, as places where great fortunes are made and lost, sometimes quickly, in such esoteric items as porkbellies, cocoa or rapeseed. Equally exotic are stories of unwitting investors being forced to take delivery of thousands of bushels of unwanted wheat because they did not properly understand the precise nature of their futures contract. Legends and myths notwithstanding, commodities do deserve their reputation as fast moving items or fast moving markets but the reasons for this are based upon simple, yet fundamental, economic factors.

A futures contract, regardless of the underlying commodity it represents, entitles the holder to buy or sell a specific amount of that commodity in a prearranged, deliverable grade at a specific date in the future at a specified price. For this contract, the individual deposits a fraction of the contract's nominal value. If, for any reason, the investor decides to terminate that contract, he may do so because commodities markets are in fact some of the most active financial markets in the world.

In addition to the future aspect of commodity markets, they differ from equity and bond markets in one other fundamental respect. In this instance, the same can also be said for foreign exchange and options markets. Futures markets are not divided into primary and secondary sectors because they do not raise capital for industry but only initiate and trade hedging positions. The initial act of creating a futures contract is the same as trading in a secondary market. The only way this phenomenon can occur is when the instrument the futures market trades is not witnessed by a certificate showing equity or a creditor status. Trading for the future is then the same as creating a position for the future and is not the same as actually possessing the commodity involved until contract delivery date.

FUNDAMENTALS OF FUTURES TRADING

The basic purpose of a futures contract is to enable individuals or companies having an interest in a commodity to hedge its price at a specified level. A manufacturer of food sauces may decide to purchase a number of contracts guaranteeing an amount of the necessary component soyabean oil of acceptable grade to be delivered to him at a specific date. In this fashion, he is protecting himself against a rise in the price of soyabean oil in the intervening period which would only erode his profit margin. Equally, the producer of the oil itself may also desire to protect himself against potential price declines in the oil which would erode his profit margin and may decide to sell forward into the futures market. Or perhaps he wants to ensure against a rise in the price of soyabeans, the basic part of his own product, and may purchase beans for a future delivery.

This simple risk aversion process does not necessarily eliminate all risks to either party. Either may agree to take delivery only to see the price of that commodity fall rather than rise, raising the possibility that their product may ultimately be too highly priced when it eventually reaches the market. Nevertheless, the basic function of the market has been fulfilled. This is the one intrinsic risk attached to any sort of hedging, however; for the insurance against price rises one also eliminates the benefits that might have accrued due to a price fall.

Futures markets also have a derivative meaning in another sense in that they are extensions of the present, or cash, markets for the commodities which they trade. How then do extensions of cash markets involving only farmers, manufacturers and producers come to affect the individual investor and have such myths attached to them? Obviously, there is a speculative element in them appealing to a wider audience than simply those involved in basic industries.

Another basic characteristic of these markets illustrates this speculative appeal. A contract for a commodity of £100,000 nominal value may be bought or sold for a very small initial deposit, perhaps only one per cent of that sum. Contracts are thus the most highly leveraged of all financial instruments. The reason for this is the present versus future cost of money. If a producer were to pay full cash for a futures position he would be deprived of the interest that that cash might have earned him, plus the lost cash flow benefits. In order to make the future delivery as feasible as possible, the cost of establishing a position must be kept as low as possible. So, commodity contracts are therefore highly leveraged and unlike most other marginable financial instruments, no interest is charged upon the debit balance. So the cost of carrying a position for either buyer or seller is the amount involved in opening it, plus the market risk attached to the position itself.

The prices of contracts parallel the price of the underlying cash commodity and it is the cash markets which give the futures markets their direction. Since the cash markets are so diverse they will have their own peculiar factors affecting supply and demand. The intensity of summer in the American midwest will affect the supply of wheat as the political situation in Ghana will affect the price of cocoa.

From the hedger's point of view, it would appear that the markets would be relatively quiet places where one would simply execute an order and then wait for the actual delivery date. However, even from the conservative hedger's position, the markets require constant monitoring to keep abreast of the multiplicity of factors which can affect market prices.

The other side of the commodity coin, speculating for price appreciation or deterioration, is also a highly specialised technique requiring elaborate knowledge of the particular commodity involved. It comprises a combination of buying and short selling. The funds provided by the speculator help to maintain liquidity on the floors of the exchanges. While hedgers generally hope for, and attempt to, hold the futures price relatively steady, speculators hope for wide price fluctuations in order to make profits. Or put another way, hedgers attempt to protect against the very phenomena speculators hope to take advantage of in the short term.

ECONOMIC ASPECTS OF FUTURES TRADING

The hedging aspect of futures trading is the primary macroeconomic function but certainly not the only economic aspect attached to the markets. Futures prices also indicate the expectations for commodity

A Guide to the Financial Markets

TABLE 4.1   Coffee futures prices (New York, September 1980)
37 500 lbs; cents per pound

year	month	open	high	low	close
1980	Sept	123.00	129.30	122.50	127.90
	Dec	129.30	134.80	128.18	133.82
1981	Mar	132.50	136.75	132.50	136.44
	May	136.99	140.00	136.50	139.47
	July	138.60	141.25	138.50	141.13
	Sept	142.00	142.00	142.00	142.75
	Dec	–	–	–	144.95

prices over the near term. In Table 4.1, prices are listed for coffee futures. As can be seen, contracts are transacted at higher prices in the longest month available than they are for the nearest month. This reflects the expectation that traders assume prices will be higher than they are presently. This does not necessarily mean that prices will be higher at those times but merely reflects expectation levels. However, the high nearby prices reflect the premium that consumers are willing to pay for coffee now and such a structure often suggests that futures prices will eventually be higher in the future.

Commodity cash prices are a vital indicator of price trends in wholesale and (eventually) retail prices. The cost of raw materials deployed in a value added process is the first link in a chain of prices eventually reaching the ultimate consumer. Thus, many commodity prices are calculated into producers' prices or wholesale prices and as such are part of a basket of component factors studied by government economists as they attempt to gauge future trends as a whole. Until the mid-1970s, this remark could have been made uncategorically but with the introduction of financial futures in the United States, it can no longer be said that all commodities are of the agricultural, farming, or metallic variety and therefore are indicators of the trend of wholesale prices.

Commodity prices are stated in the same terms as foreign exchange prices in that the cash price today is referred to as the *spot price* while the futures are always differentiated. In market terminology, if the future price is below the spot, the price is said to stand at a *discount*, while if it is higher, it stands at a *premium*. Forward discounts are also known in more technical language as a state of *backwardation*, while forward premiums are referred to as *contangos*. The former means that expectation levels in the future are low. The latter, a term also seen when we discussed British stock market techniques, means that expectations are optimistic. These two terms can and have been applied to any similar economic situation even if commodities or British shares are not being discussed.[1]

It should not be automatically assumed that contangos are necessarily a *sine qua non* of healthy economic conditions while backwardations are strictly anomalous. If contangos generally characterised the price of sugar over a two year period, obviously the price of all sugar related items would also be higher, suggesting price inflation. Similarly, constant backwardation suggests price deflation and neither condition is conducive to economic prosperity in itself.

Neither should it be assumed that all futures prices are necessarily indicative of future expectations. As can be seen in Table 4.1, futures do have different delivery dates. Most are spread out over three month intervals so that the hedger can choose the month in which he wants to take delivery. Speculators, however, may not necessarily feel that all future contract months are equally viable in speculative terms and therefore may avoid certain contracts. Although the general principle applies that in most situations, arbitrageurs will level anomalous prices, the cost of money plus technical conditions surrounding certain contract months can be a serious consideration which can detract from the generalisation that *all* futures prices are indicative of expectation levels.

One somewhat infamous characteristic of the markets is their putative price volatility. This reputation stems from the fact that one tick (small movement) in price can mean several thousand pounds or dollars when large numbers of contracts are being traded. From the hedger's point of view, this is natural since he may be dealing in contracts representing several tonnes of a particular commodity. On the speculator's side, however, this volatility can be quite costly or profitable, and it is from the speculator's side that the myths surrounding the market normally originate.

As an example, imagine that a widgetbar contract represents 50 000 pounds of widgetbars and is worth, in nominal terms, $1 million. If the contract is trading at par then each pound of widgetbars is worth $20. In order to trade this contract, the individual must place a deposit representing 0.5% of the nominal value, or $5 000. Now, if the price of widgetbars fluctuates by only 1% (2 cents on the original price of $20 per pound) the investor stands to make, or lose, $10 000 on his original deposit of $5 000. While this would appear to be relatively insignificant to the producer or manufacturer needing 100 tonnes of the commodity it is a different matter to a speculator who might have miscalculated on the price direction of widgetbars. The volatility involved is to be expected when such large amounts of materials, highly geared, are being traded.

MARKET MECHANICS AND TECHNIQUES

Basic market technique is essentially the same for all commodities, regardless of the market in which they are traded. Normally, only procedural matters are different.[2] The two fundamental techniques are both integral to hedging and are known as the *long* and *short* hedges. The long hedge has already been described here above. The short variety utilises short selling to protect prices from downward deterioration.

Just as the long hedge attempts to lock in a future price level for those desirous of owning that particular commodity in point of time, the short hedge does the same but in this case the short sale normally hedges either the physical commodity itself or a long position in contracts. This is shown in Figure 4.1. A manufacturer already holds ten contracts of widgetbars but does not want to see their price deteriorate; a risk pointed out earlier here. In order to protect the position, he then shorts an equal amount of contracts at a similar price to that he originally paid and he is effectively hedged. The theory is quite simple but the actual practice sounds somewhat peculiar at first glance. If cash prices fall so does the value of the long contracts. The manufacturer will then be faced with incorporating expensive widgetbars into his process when they could have been obtained more cheaply. But perhaps more importantly, a subsequent drop in price will also adversely affect his margin position since he is responsible for drops in price before actual delivery date and must maintain contract margin as well. Calls on his position can only

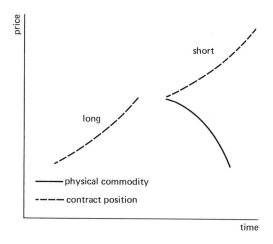

FIGURE 4.1   Long and short hedging

cost him money in point of time plus paperwork. In order to prevent such occurrences, a short hedge may be the viable answer. Using the hedge, the short will gain what the long loses, thereby keeping his position even. As mentioned earlier, this type of hedge, as with all hedges in general, eliminates potential profits as it does losses if the cash price should suddenly move.

Since hedging aids in reducing risk it is obviously the basic tool used by many directly involved in the production processes. Short selling is also a tool used by the prudent and should not only be assumed to be a technique employed by the trader. The methods employed by the speculator, or scalper as he is sometimes known, use the same two basic tools in other combinations to achieve a quite different purpose.

Speculators will use the long and short positions, or a combination of the two, with one essential difference from the hedger: in no instance does the speculator actually desire delivery of the commodities involved. They intend to close out their positions before the deadline date for delivery is reached. This factor ensures that the nearest delivery month will be quite actively traded and price discrepancies are less likely in them than in the later dated contracts. The speculator's strategies, other than an outright long or short position, are, therefore, forms of price arbitrage spread out over time. Hence the name for these types of activities – *spreading*.

Financial markets terminology can be imprecise at times and the nomenclature attached to time/price arbitrage is one glaring example. Spreading means the practice of buying a contract in one delivery month and selling another of the same commodity in a different delivery month. At the same time, it could mean a long and a short position in different commodities practically related. For instance, a trader knows that the normal price differential between soyabeans and soyabean oil is normally x. This is due to the fact that the oil is the product of the bean. If he sees the price fall out of line he is apt to go long one and short the other. This procedure will eventually bring prices back into line, as it will in any arbitrage process.

This latter inter-commodity spread is sometimes referred to as a *straddle* but this term is not precise. A straddle is actually the short hedge described earlier whereby the investor seeks to straddle the current price by going long and short simultaneously, or by having one leg over each side of the fence in less elegant language. Straddling in this sense could be between futures and a cash position or more theoretically, between two futures positions. It should be noted that the term straddle in United States market parlance refers to a spread in a commodity other than

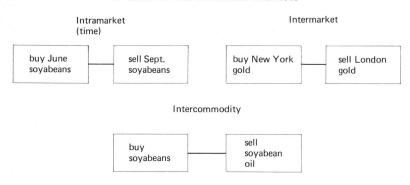

FIGURE 4.2   Types of spreading

grains. Figure 4.2 illustrates each process under the single term of spreading.

The time spread attempts to lock in a gain from a price anomaly which the trader feels has risen between contract months. In Table 4.1, there is a premium discrepancy between the two delivery dates. In order to take advantage of this, the trader buys the near month and shorts the long month. If his assumption that the long month was too expensive proves true, others will also follow suit. Purchases in the short month will cause a price rise as a result and sales in the long month will cause price declines. Then the trader reverses (and closes) his position, taking the profit. In more technical jargon, the contango proved short lived and the ensuing arbitrage created a narrower position between the two months.

Spreading is an activity witnessed in other financial markets, namely bond and options markets in addition to commodities.[3] It is an arbitrage technique with one additional element of risk attached – time. However, it still meets the acid test for arbitrage set out in Chapter 1 in that it involves the levelling in price of instruments which are economic substitutes (in this case, the same instrument). But the question the process raises is somewhat more complex: is a commodity contract maturing in month 1 an economic substitute for the same commodity contract maturing in month 2?

The answer to this question is negative but it should be kept in mind that commodity markets are not capital markets but futures markets and, therefore, the precise definition set out in Chapter 1 concerning arbitrage requires a further qualification. In forward markets, arbitrage can *only* be (in its simplest sense) between contract dates rather than physical assets insofar as the speculator is concerned. There is no other substitute for June wheat or December gold. If delivery of the actual commodity itself is used to force this hypothetical issue it quickly becomes apparent that no other alternative can exist. Thus, commodity futures arbitrage is normally confined to activities between contract months, unless a straight straddle is deemed necessary for whatever reason.

If commodity contract months are read in a linear manner then it can be seen that their prices form their own version of the yield curve. Table 4.1 is reconstructed in this manner in Figure 4.3. We have already noted some of the pitfalls involved in assuming that all futures prices are accurate reflections of investor expectations but, nevertheless, this commodity 'curve' is all that is currently available by which one can gauge the future.

There is one peculiarity concerning all futures trading, whether it be in commodities, foreign exchange, or options, which should be noted because without an understanding of the basic concept a serious gap exists in the knowledge of anyone attempting to understand these markets. This concerns the creation of the actual position itself. As noted earlier, there is no distinction between primary and secondary markets in the futures arenas. And since no actual securities are involved, commodity contracts are created by investor desire alone. This is the heart of what is known in all the futures markets as *certificateless trading*. The position itself is only a book-keeping entry on the books of

FIGURE 4.3   Term structure of forward coffee prices

the broker or bank involved. No securities of any sort are involved and futures contracts, therefore, do not have the same status as actual securities in that they may not be hypothecated, or used for collateral.

The long hedger opening a position actually creates an *open position* in the month he trades. When the short seller initially sells, the same is true. The amount of *open interest*, or actual positions outstanding, is limited only by investor interest. If on a certain day ten individual investors desire to open ten positions each, 100 new contracts will be added to the amount of open interest for that particular month. Theoretically, the total amount is limitless.[4]

Of course, this assumes that for each individual seeking to open a position there is a counterpart somewhere in the market. In most instances, the counter-party is a floor trader or scalper having access to the exchange floor. Since commodities are traded in auction fashion, any number of counterparties may be available at any one time to provide the necessary liquidity.

The high gearing levels available to speculators are also advantageous to the hedger. For the scalper, it is possible to take a profit from a very small price movement. The quick actions of this group tend to ensure adequate price levels during the course of a day so that hedging functions may be performed. But this is not to imply that risk under even normal circumstances is not present. The low margin levels on contracts concomitantly means that price movements will have a more severe impact upon both types of investor. In many cases, price movements on one day could present the contract holder with an amount greater than his original deposit.

Since the actual deposit is small, the debt amount (that is, the difference between the deposit and the actual value of the contract) is quite large. Unlike some stock market practices, the debit amount is not charged interest. Nevertheless, a maintenance margin is calculated daily so that investors who are on the losing side of a position, even briefly, are liable to margin calls in order to maintain equity in the position. Leverage in this case does not imply license in that losses must be acknowledged and partially paid even before the contract is finally closed.

Due to price volatility, commodity contracts have what is known as *limit movements* built into their trading mechanics. These limits are administered by the commodities exchanges. If a particular contract moves *limit up*, this means that it must trade at or below that particular price for the remainder of that trading day before seeking a new level the next day. Conversely, *limit down* means that a maximum price fall has been established, again for that particular day only. The virtue of these maximum price movement levels is that they protect the investor from deleterious movements occurring too quickly.

TYPES OF COMMODITIES

Regardless of the locale in which they are traded, commodities can be broken into several general types – agricultural products, agricultural by-products, metals and financial instruments. There are several subdivisions in each category, depending upon the country in which the respective markets are located. And if some of the names of commodities in the next section should sound somewhat peculiar, it should be kept in mind that contracts represent basic commodities used in a variety of final products. Many times these commodities are not household words.

Most commodity futures traded on the exchanges today provide a perceptual problem for those not actually engaged in trade involving the particular commodities themselves. Unlike equities or bonds, they do not represent securities of a company which themselves can be studied and scrutinised for investment potential. More fundamentally, they represent the basic goods used by many of those companies in their businesses. In this sense, commodity markets represent a much more basic type of activity than equity or bond markets.

For this very reason, no detailed description will be attempted here of the multitudinous commodities traded on the world markets since they are so diverse. However, one new type of commodity contract initiated in the late 1970s in Chicago does bear some attention both for its innovative nature plus the impact it is having upon the traditional money and bond markets. And neither does it fit the traditional generic classification of either *hard* or *soft* commodity because it is a contract representing a financial instrument.

In 1976, financial futures were introduced on the Chicago commodity exchanges. Initially, contracts represented nominal amounts of United States Treasury bills and bonds as well. These contracts represented the right to take delivery of bills or bonds of a stated yield level at three-month intervals. They attempted to give the financial manager and speculator the same edge given to producers and manufacturers. But in this instance what was being hedged were short- and long-term interest rates rather than traditional commodities.

Originally, interest rate futures were designed to be used as any other commodity contract but because of the diverse nature of treasury bills and bonds the matter of settling upon what is known as deliverable grade bills and bonds became a pivotal issue.[5] If one were required to deliver coffee against a forward position, the quality of that coffee is stipulated by the contract. But in the case of financial futures, the problem is more complex. This is due in part to the nature of the financial contracts themselves. For instance, the treasury bond contract is based upon a notional 8% 20-year bond. In reality, this coupon and maturity level can only be used as a benchmark for long-term interest rates in general since there are many more government bonds in existence with both higher coupons and longer maturities. Thus, any one of several approved cash bonds are deliverable against a contract in any one given month.

Hedging using bond and bill futures is then not so much a matter of the actual contract in physical terms as much as it is what it represents in yield level terms. It is possible to hedge a $10\frac{3}{8}$% 30 year bond by using the benchmark contract if the cash and futures position are both at a similar yield level. In practice, this means that the contract will be at a deeper discount or smaller premium than the bond because its coupon level is $2\frac{3}{8}$% lower.

Both long and short hedging were designed to help financial managers, portfolio managers and others who needed interest rate protection for their portfolio holdings, either at present or in the near future.

A portfolio manager with $10 million invested in long bonds with an average yield of 10% may decide that he requires protection against a rise in long rates by going short a similar amount of bond futures. By shorting at the proper level, he is then locked into his desired yield. If rates should rise by 1%, his portfolio will lose in value but his hedge should gain and vice versa. As with all short hedging techniques, the primary opportunity which is lost through this strategy is the possibility that long-term rates will decline. In this case, the loss on the hedge will offset any gain the bond positions may have accumulated.

The long hedge is simply used to lock in today's yields for the future by purchasing contracts. This strategy is only valid if the buyer thinks that rates will decline in the future. Nevertheless, both strategies (Figure 4.4) are being increasingly used by prudent investors desiring to hedge against interest rate uncertainty. When these contracts were introduced in 1976–77, trading developed rather slowly because US interest rates were relatively stable. But in the summer of 1978, an inverse yield curve developed and persisted for almost two years before again assuming a

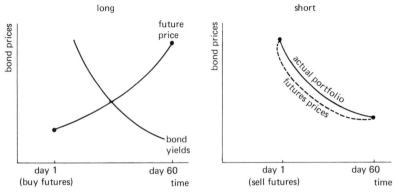

FIGURE 4.4   Financial futures hedges

normal slope. During that period, many bond holdings suffered huge paper and real losses. As a result, hedging techniques received an inadvertent boost from the money and bond markets themselves. Currently, trading in some contract months in treasury bills actually exceeds the amount of bills outstanding; that is, the open interest is greater than the actual cash value of bills outstanding.

In this respect, critics of the financial futures markets maintain that speculation in bill and bond futures may actually damage the Treasury's ability to auction debt since many potential bidders have an outlet in the futures markets. The speculative appeal, plus the low margin deposit, are possibly siphoning off liquidity from the cash market. While this question is certainly moot for present purposes, it should be noted that it does pose a cognate question which anyone who studies the futures or forward markets should bear in mind: do potentially limitless contract positions have any effect upon the cash markets upon which they are based?

This question will arise again in Chapter 6 concerning options because in that certificateless market, open interest may be added simply by initiating a contract position. Whether or not these seemingly limitless positions do affect the underlying instruments for better or worse can only be answered by empirical research, but one or two comments can, nevertheless, be made in general terms.

On the negative side, it could well be argued that the cash markets are suffering a lack of potential liquidity at the hands of the futures markets, but this position is based upon one assumption which is quite hard to verify; namely, that all futures traders are potential cash purchasers. From patterns developing in the financial futures sector, it appears that most, although certainly not all, positions are closed before actual delivery date. This suggests that most hedgers do not desire delivery of the instrument but are merely content with the hedging opportunities afforded by the contract during its life span. Thus, they are content to hedge, or speculate, using the high leverage factor without actually considering actual physical delivery. This argument would appear to be mixing apples and oranges by assuming that all hedgers or speculators are actually investors in bills or bonds in sheep's clothing.

On the positive side, it can be argued that the futures markets have added an element of stability to the cash markets by getting the speculators off the streets and into the betting parlours where they belong, in a manner of speaking. Again, the leverage factor is crucial to this position. Government obligations may be traded on margin (normally five per cent of total value) but the cost of carrying such paper depends upon the federal funds rate and the REPO (repurchase agreement) rate. Futures obviously provide more attraction to this sort of financing since they require only about a two per cent deposit and no funding costs.

Regardless of one's views concerning the financial futures markets, they are, nevertheless, becoming parallel markets to the cash markets because they are offering the opportunity to hedge risks which are becoming more and more severe under current international and domestic inflationary conditions, as well as changing domestic monetary policies. In this respect, they bear something of an analogy with the British parallel money market in that, while the latter was not the traditional avenue for banks to follow in satisfying reserve requirements, it nevertheless grew into a viable tool to be utilised. This is not to imply that a forward market can act as surrogate for money or bond markets, but merely underscores their importance in a rapidly changing financial environment.

THE BRITISH AND AMERICAN MARKETS

Both marketplaces have their origins in the nineteenth century when farmers and traders first organised to protect themselves against future price fluctuations. Prior to that time, commodity (cash or physical) markets were an established fixture of many European economies and were the predecessors of many of today's stock exchanges.

The markets themselves are quite diverse; some trade many types of futures contracts while others tend to specialise in certain types of commodities only. The markets and their specialities can be found in

Table 4.2 British commodity futures markets

market	commodities traded
London Commodity Exchange	tea, coffee, cocoa, sugar, vegetable oils, spices, rubber
London Metal Exchange	tin, lead, copper, zinc, silver
London Grain Futures Market	grain
London Silver Market	silver (physicals and futures)
London Gold Market	gold (physicals only)
Liverpool Commodities Exchange	cotton, corn

Tables 4.2 and 4.3. It can be seen that the two sectors have factors in common and quite different types of contracts, reflecting the products of the domestic economies as well as the basic imports upon which each relies.

Despite their seeming diversities, all commodity markets share one common trait differentiating them from forward markets discussed in the next chapter. Regardless of location, size or nature of the commodity traded, all commodity markets in Britain and the United States are linked domestically to each other by a clearing house. The clearing house is an institution which performs the basic backroom functions of the markets in aggregate, such as matching of orders consummated on

Table 4.3 American commodity futures markets

market	commodities traded
Chicago Board of Trade	oats, corn, soyabeans, soy oil, soy meal, iced broilers, plywood, lumber, wheat, financial futures
Chicago Mercantile Exchange	currency futures, live hogs, pork bellies, live cattle, feeder cattle, eggs, lumber, sorghum, potatoes
New York Cocoa Exchange	cocoa
New York Cotton Exchange	cotton, orange juice, propane
New York Coffee and Sugar Exchange	coffee, sugar
Commodity Exchange, Inc.	copper, gold
International Monetary Market	silver coins (US and Canadian), gold, currencies
New York Mercantile Exchange	gold, platinum, palladium, potatoes, silver coins
New York Futures Exchange	financial futures

the exchange floors and allocating call notices and delivery notices. But the fundamental economic function of the clearing house is to insure all contracts against failure to deliver. In this respect, the clearing house assumes the ultimate risk of providing orderly functioning markets for its members.

As tables 4.2 and 4.3 illustrate, the two sectors do share some commodities in common, perhaps the best known being gold. Arbitrage does occur between the trans-Atlantic markets from time to time as it does between the individual domestic markets but it hinges upon several factors. First, the deliverable grade of the commodity must, in fact, be similar. Otherwise, actual delivery from one market to another would not be feasible. Second, arbitraging for small price discrepancies between the two might not always be practical due to communications costs or actual delivery costs and there may, at times, be price lag differentials between markets on the same trading day.

NOTES

1. See for example J. Hicks, *Value and Capital*, 2nd ed. (Oxford University Press, 1978) ch. 10 and J. M. Keynes, *Treatise on Money* (London: Macmillan, 1930).
2. For the contrast between British and American commodity procedures see T. Watling and J. Morley, *Successful Commodity Futures Trading*, 2nd ed. (London: Business Books, 1978) and F. Horn and V. Farrah, *Trading in Commodity Futures*, 2nd ed. (New York Institute of Finance, 1979).
3. In bond markets, traders 'butterfly' the yield curve between different maturity dates to determine whether there is any discrepancy in yields. In the options markets, traders also 'butterfly' different striking prices to take advantage of anomalies.
4. Open interest is the amount of contracts open and neither closed out by a corresponding position nor by taking actual delivery. It is calculated by adding up either the total amount of open long or short positions, but not both.
5. In addition to treasury bill and bond contracts, the Chicago markets also trade contracts in commercial paper, certificates of deposit, and Government National Mortgage Association (Ginnie Mae) certificates.

SUGGESTED READING

Frederick Horne and V. Farrah, *Trading in Commodity Futures*, 2nd ed. (New York Institute of Finance, 1979).

S. Kroll and I. Shisko, *The Commodity Futures Market Guide* (New York: Harper and Row, 1973).

T. Watling and J. Morley, *Successful Commodity Futures Trading*, 2nd ed. (London: Business Books, 1978).

B. A. Goss and B. S. Yamey (eds), *The Economics of Futures Trading* (London: Macmillan, 1976, 2nd ed. 1978).

5 Foreign Exchange Markets

Of all the financial markets, perhaps the least visible to the public eye is the worldwide network of banks comprising the foreign exchange markets. For most individuals, the only time that they will come into contact with it is when they buy foreign currencies for a holiday abroad. Nevertheless, this international market is one of the largest financial markets in the world; a vital tool for international business which has a constant appetite for diverse currencies and a commensurate need to hedge its foreign exchange liabilities.

Foreign exchange (forex) is probably the oldest of all the financial markets although, as commodity futures markets, they have only existed in their present form since the beginning of the century. As international business has grown so has the forex market since multinational corporations are the main customers of its services. The market has changed its complexion alongside rapidly changing developments in international commerce. And perhaps no other financial market has been quite as sensitive to political events since it has developed its present character in response to occurrences in the international monetary system following the first world war. But it has been developments since the second war which have had the most formidable impact upon its character.

Understanding the ambiance and role of the foreign exchange markets, therefore, requires a grasp of the international events which gave the market its current direction. Anyone who travelled fifteen years ago may remember that purchasing sterling with US dollars was a relatively cut and dried matter since sterling's value did not fluctuate much and, therefore, one could be assured of the general rate of exchange, within a narrow range, in advance. Today, however, the traveller may find himself or herself susceptible to quite wide exchange rate movements which can severely affect purchasing power within a short period. The reasons for this change are quite labyrinthine, and functional or technical explanations alone are not suitable if they ignore the international developments causing such a far reaching structural change in the market.

Before discussing in outline form the major changes in the international monetary system since 1945, the basic economic role of the forex market needs to be mentioned so that one can develop a grasp of the reasons for mitigating risk in the market and how this situation is rapidly changing.

Any enterprise engaged in international trade, whether it be a corporation, government or quasi-sovereign enterprise, incurs an *economic exposure* when it either converts its native currency into a foreign one, or incurs a liability in a foreign currency which later needs to be converted. This risk can be divided into many varieties, depending upon the nature of the organisations involved, but essentially the exposure is of three general types, *accounting exposure*, *short-term economic exposure* and *long-term economic exposure*. Accounting exposure will be included here although some will maintain that it is not economic exposure *per se*. However, for introductory purposes it will be included. Each type of exposure can be treated differently in financial accounts and will have a different impact upon the organisation in turn. Accounting exposure is probably the most visible of the three in the short term. For instance, if a company sells a portion of its product overseas and receives revenues in a foreign currency, any downward movement in that particular currency will have a negative impact upon earnings. Equally, any valuation of foreign assets during the same period will have a negative impact upon financial statements and perhaps even upon the stock market capitalisation of a company should investors read this as a negative sign for the parent company itself.

Regardless of the type of exposure or risk one centres upon, the monetary history of the last thirty-five years provides an excellent backdrop against which one can develop an appreciation for the intrinsic risks of dealing in foreign exchange.

FROM BRETTON WOODS TO SMITHSONIAN

After 1919, many countries adopted what is known as the gold exchange standard, a variation of the gold standard that previously existed. According to this benchmark, a country's foreign exchange reserves were kept in the currency of a country which was backed by gold. This was a post-war variation of the older gold standard when all countries able to do so attempted to back their currencies with gold. However, inflation of domestic money stocks made the direct standard obsolete and reserve assets were then sought in those currencies wealthy enough to maintain a gold backing. This is the origin of the term 'hard currency' although it has a different connotation today.

This system survived intact, some devaluations and revaluations notwithstanding, until the advent of the Bretton Woods (New Hampshire) Conference in 1944, designed to construct an international payments system applicable after the war finally ended. The Conference established, *inter alia*, the International Monetary Fund (IMF), an organisation comprised of member states to help facilitate the envisaged new payments system. Some of the Conference's other measures were destined to lead to eventual volatility in the foreign exchange markets as a result of a return to the gold standard in order to establish parities for the international currencies. Indirectly, this meant that currencies would be linked to the US dollar since it was linked to gold for official statement purposes.

The parity level of the currency of each IMF member, when established, had the net effect of allowing them to fluctuate within a very narrow range except for a revaluation (marking upwards) or devaluation (marking downwards) of a currency with prior IMF approval. Currencies were allowed to 'float' within a very narrow range of only 1 per cent on either side of their established parities. Beyond these levels, the central bank of the respective country would have to intervene to maintain the rate. If the currency was falling because there were more sellers than buyers on the forex market, the bank involved would be required to intervene by buying it to shore it up against depreciation. Conversely, if it rose up against its upper limits a bank would be required to increase the supply on the market in order to bring its price down within required limits.

The Conference also spelt out definite procedures for a new valuation of a currency; that is, its upward revaluation or downward devaluation outside its parity levels. Only a disequilibrium in a country's balance of payments could cause a situation whereby a currency had to be realigned. This meant that new valuations were *official* in that they had to follow accepted guidelines.

This apparent stability in the day to day maintenance of exchange rates does not imply that the system was necessarily successful because in the end it bore the seeds of its own destruction. Because of the parity link with gold, and concomitantly with the US dollar, that currency officially became the concern of international investors everywhere.

Beginning in the 1950s and taking on impetus in the 1960s, the dollar began to flow out of the United States in increasing amounts as American influence and investment abroad spread. Following this, increasing demand for the dollar as a transaction currency spread. The net result was that the United States began to run sizeable balance of payments deficits.

The dollar maintained its own levels during this time although many other currencies were forced to devalue in point of time, notably France (1957, 1958, 1969) and Britain (1967). Equally, many also found themselves in the position of revaluing themselves during the same general period, notably Germany (1969) and Holland (1961). One of the major results of the large outflows of dollars from the mainland was the formation of the eurodollar market in the early 1960s as many dollar balances were being held in accounts outside the mainland United States. These were held by many types of depositors, from individuals to corporations and central banks, holding their dollar assets in a non-American centre in order to take advantage of high interest rates. At this time, under managed floating rates, or fixed rates as they actually were, currency swings were often not great enough to take advantage of in the short run and many depositors were content to stay invested in dollars and not switch to other currencies in order to gain a short-term trading profit.

The end of the Bretton Woods system came in 1971 when the convertibility of the dollar into gold was terminated and the dollar began to float. Another conference was held at the Smithsonian Institute where a new regime of currency parity was established. The old band of 1 per cent was widened to allow currencies to float within a range of $2\frac{1}{4}$ per cent of parity, and the price of gold was raised $3 per ounce to $38, effectively devaluing the dollar by about 8 per cent.

In 1973 the Smithsonian arrangement came to a halt as the price of gold was again increased by 10 per cent following further balance of payments deficits in the United States and the dollar devalued by a further 10 per cent. Currencies were no longer officially pegged to the dollar in any fashion and they were left to float freely to find their own levels.

Despite the demise of the Bretton Woods and Smithsonian systems, foreign exchange patois is still replete with terms originating in the earlier part of the century, today having somewhat different connotations. The term *hard currency* is still used but now refers to currencies backed by a large amount of foreign reserves in the coffers, rather than gold. *Convertibility* is also used but no longer means the ability to convert the currency into gold. Today it means that the currency is freely convertible on the forex markets into other currencies. Currently, most of the currencies of the industrialised countries are convertible while those of the third world are not.

Central bank intervention in the market is still necessary in order to protect currencies against too rapid rises or falls and the speculation which invariably accompanies such situations. Often, rapid change in a currency's value, following a rise in domestic interest rates, can be directly attributed to central bank shifting of funds, for reasons that will become clearer later.

The dollar is the major reserve currency today. This means that countries prefer to hold their reserves in dollars either because a good proportion of their trade is done in dollars or because there exists no viable substitute. The Deutschmark is second in importance, followed by sterling which has slipped from its position of pre-eminence since the 1967 devaluation (Table 5.1). How these reserve currencies are manipulated by their central bank holders can severely affect the money market in the United States, the euromarket and, indirectly, Switzerland, West Germany and the United Kingdom among others. For instance, if a country holds $1 billion in reserves, it will obviously seek to place them in instruments both highly liquid and slightly less liquid if possible, which will give the highest return on its investment.[1] Normally the usual outlets for dollar reserves are United States Treasury bills and bonds, eurodollar term deposits and, in some cases, eurodollar bonds.

Prudent portfolio management by a central bank dictates that a large proportion of these reserves must be placed in liquid money market instruments. If the rates on eurodollar term deposits are higher than those on US Treasury bills, the eurodollar market will be the recipient until such time as a swing occurs back to the domestic market. The same

TABLE 5.1   Composition of IMF members' reserves (SDR billions)

currency	1976	1977	1978	1979 (June)
US dollar	152	190	205	211
Deutschmark	4	6	8	8
pound sterling	3	3	3	3
others	1	1	1	1
total	160	200	217	223

SOURCE: IMF *Survey*

is true of the relationship between United States Treasury bonds and eurodollar bonds. Central bank shifting in times of interest rate volatility can have a profound impact upon the markets involved.

It should not be assumed that *all* reserves will be left in dollars and invested in dollar instruments simply because the country in question does a large proportion of its international trade in dollars. The central bank may decide to diversify into other currencies. Imagine five countries with $1 billion reserves each, all of which trade with the United States and which decide to shift twenty per cent of their reserves into Deutschmarks. This represents $1 billion worth of buying power on the forex markets and if all of them decide to diversify at the same time, they could have a serious impact upon the rates for both the dollar and the mark. It is quite conceivable that a concerted action here to buy marks would eventually require the German central bank (Bundesbank) to intervene in order to keep the mark at acceptable levels. At the same time, the Federal Reserve would have had to intervene to prop up the dollar against selling pressures. If the mark appreciated too much against the dollar, the value of German exports would increase which, if left unchecked, would reduce the foreign demand for German export goods and have a negative impact upon the balance of trade. In order to intervene, the Bundesbank would have to sell Deutschmarks into the market to satisfy demand. If the only way to accomplish this was to print more marks, then the money stock would also become inflated.

Dollar instability over the last decade has caused occasional havoc on the foreign exchanges and the net effect extends far beyond central bank activities. At the same time that central banks are forming their strategies, hundreds of multinational corporations worldwide are also having the same strategy sessions and the amount of money to support a consensus view could easily be multiplied severalfold, causing serious consequences. In order to mitigate the deleterious or unknown consequences of currency fluctuations, organisations turn to the foreign exchange markets to hedge their risks.[2]

ECONOMICS OF FOREIGN EXCHANGE TRADING

As mentioned, the exposure of being susceptible to currency fluctuations is threefold. In addition to the accountancy risk (the impact of exchange movements upon profit and loss statements and balance sheets), two other types of economic exposure are also evident – the short- and long-term. Although there are certainly more sub-categories depending upon the type of organisation discussed, these are the general types prevalent.[3]

So that these risks are made as clear as possible they will be described here in investment terms rather than in corporate finance language. Accounting risk, however, is not so easily translated into individual investor language.

Currency fluctuations will have a volatile impact upon company accounts by keeping them in a constant state of flux. The task of deciding whether a company is profitable or not takes on an added dimension insofar as the investor is concerned. However, any company dealing in foreign exchange knows how to hedge itself and this is not the main thrust of the problem with currency fluctuations. When floating rates are combined with stringent accounting rules, the impact upon a company can be quite serious.

In the United States an accounting practice was used during the mid and latter 1970s which provides an example. The Financial Accounting Standards Board required that all foreign subsidiaries of United States companies included in the parent company's financial statements value their fixed assets (in the appropriate foreign currency) using a historical valuation; that is, its worth in dollars using the appropriate exchange rate at time of purchase. At the time of subsequent financial statements, the books of the parent could therefore show volatile swings, depending upon the dollar's exchange performance as it affected the value of the subsidiary in relation to the parent. This rule, known as FAS 8, had a serious impact upon quarterly earnings reports and consequent stock market reaction to shares.

The difference between short- and long-term exposure is obviously the amount of time involved and, for practical purposes, they can be described in the same general manner. However, it should be noted that there are different techniques of hedging such exposures but in some cases the long term is the more vulnerable of the two because long hedging techniques are more difficult.

Borrowing upon examples already used in other chapters, imagine an investor who has a large amount of dollars to invest. He does not necessarily want to place them in United States dollar bonds because the highest yield he can obtain is 11%. At the same time, British gilts are yielding 14% and he finds this an appealing return. But in order to buy sterling with his dollars (so that he can buy the gilts) he will incur a foreign exchange risk; namely, the present value of the dollar versus the pound for the time that he remains invested in gilts.

The amount of risk is diluted somewhat by the 3% differential that exists between the American and British bonds. This is referred to as an *interest rate differential* although it is not normally measured by comparing bond yields. We will return to this point momentarily. In other words, the investor can suffer a 3 per cent depreciation of the pound against the dollar before he actually loses money. This is shown diagrammatically in Figure 5.1. If the pound is purchased at $2.40 then the 14% yield will be true at the end of the investment period only if the investor can repurchase dollars at $2.40 or more. Put another way, his incurred liability is in sterling and that currency must remain at current levels or appreciate when he again decides to purchase dollars.

Broadening this perspective, imagine a corporation that invests money in a foreign subsidiary, assuming that after two or three years the investment will return an amount sufficient to offset the initial amount invested, plus make a small profit. The revenues will be in a foreign currency although the company will have to value these assets and revenues in its native currency. Any downward depreciation in that currency, below the value on the day it was purchased, will involve a twofold loss; the valuation of the investment itself, plus the depreciated revenues it produces.

The question normally arising here is whether both individual and corporation could not hedge themselves by selling their currency exposure forward for delivery at the same time they want to return to their native currencies. As far as the corporation is concerned, the answer is 'yes' in that it could hedge the amount of the actual investment itself, assuming that it had to be repaid to a lender in full in two or three years' time. In the case of the investor, the answer is 'no'. Unlike commodity hedges, forex hedges are more complex because of the international nature of the currencies themselves. If the gilt investor had sold sterling forward it would have had the net effect of reducing his effective interest rate received back to the dollar level. The reason for this seeming paradox is to be found in international interest rate differentials and how the foreign exchange markets react to them.

FIGURE 5.1   US *v.* UK interest rate differential

MECHANICS OF FOREIGN EXCHANGE TRADING

Before attempting to resolve this forward selling problem, the basic techniques of the market need to be discussed because, although they are similar to commodity market techniques, some of the terminology varies. The basic distinction drawn in the last chapter between commodity markets and foreign exchange markets should also be reiterated here; forex markets are over-the-counter markets conducted by international banks and do not have a central location. Neither do they have a clearing house performing settlement functions for them so there is no third party to ensure the transaction is completed by the client and agent. And in less functional language, forex markets are referred to as *forward markets* rather than futures markets.

The activities of banks, corporations and governments are dictated by the need to hedge risks but one not so obvious twist is also present here. The market makers themselves also seek to reduce their own exposure, brought about by transacting business for others, by dealing in the forward markets as well. Since there is a fine line between international economic developments and actual market mechanics, it can appear that market techniques are nothing more than reactions to international monetary trends, which, of course, they are.

When exchange rates were more stable prior to the collapse of the Bretton Woods system, the general theory of exchange rate movements in the future was somewhat static in that forward rates were thought simply to be a reflection of the expectations of market participants. If the forward rate was at a premium to the cash, or *spot*, rate then obviously participants thought the currency would appreciate in the future. But with the advent of floating rates this theory gave way to a more dynamic theory as dictated by real interest rate differentials. The idea behind this is quite simple: in our original example above, the rate differential between the United States and the United Kingdom is 3% so, therefore, the pound will be at a 3% forward discount to the dollar.[4] But a comparison of the domestic rates is not as germane as a comparison of similar euro-rates for the two currencies which may vary from the domestic differential comparison.

Returning to the example, it now becomes apparent why our investor could not sell sterling forward in order to short hedge his exposure. In order to do so, he would have had to sell it forward at a lower rate than that at which he purchased it; an anomaly in a dynamic market which reacts to differentials. Where forward premiums do incongruously appear, they normally disappear again quickly as arbitrageurs narrow the differentials.

Since the differential between bonds was 3%, we can assume that the pound will be at a 3% forward discount to the dollar. So if the investor sold forward he would immediately lose 3 per cent on the currency and be back at the 11% bond rate, a return to United States interest rates that he was trying to better in the first place.

International interest rate differentials are immediately contingent upon domestic rate differentials, themselves tied somewhat imperfectly to the domestic inflation rate. But more often, the euromarket rates spell the differential between forex forward rates since this market is more readily accessible to international investors. Although many countries have now abolished exchange controls, the euromarket remains the only place where most convertible currencies can be acquired regardless of domestic restrictions. Thus, forward margins are more likely to reflect eurocurrency rate differentials than they are domestic differentials. This is shown in Table 5.2.

Although eurodollar rates are necessarily higher than their domestic counterparts due to the market's expatriate character, the differentials between any two currency sectors should be in about the same proportion as the difference in domestic rates. And all the differentials are based upon a common but diverse number of factors which affect the interest rate spread in the first place, such as domestic inflation, the current account and trade balances, as well as the overall outlook for the economy and currency itself.

If our original investor had followed through on the differentials and

TABLE 5.2   Dollar forward margin and eurocurrency differential

	3 month interest rate		spot (bid-offer)	exchange rate	
				3 month forward	
	% p.a.	Δ*		margin	% p.a.
interest rates					
euro $	18				
euro Can. $	17	−1			
euro £	15	−3			
exchange rate					
US $–£			2.3850–2.3860	1.97–1.87 pm†	3.22
US $–Can. $			1.1660–1.1665	0.32–0.27 pm	1.01

* difference between relevant rate and euro $ rate
† premium. Margins usually refer to the dollar value of other currency.

purchased sterling, he would have incurred the full exchange risk less the 3% differential. Many other investors also engage in uncovered foreign currency investment when they find that normal investment vehicles in their own countries do not exceed the inflation rate. This is referred to as a negative real rate of return because the yield does not exceed inflation and the investor is not gaining in real terms. Many then are willing to look abroad for a real rate even if it means incurring risk.

This real rate of return has far reaching consequences in the international financial markets in general and is a powerful force behind foreign exchange and money market movements because it normally applies to those international investors desirous of shifting a mix of convertible currencies around in favour of the highest rate of return available. It is not as true of domestic investors who require their own currency for payments and protection of assets and liabilities denominated in that currency. Floating exchange rates have spawned dynamic markets, in themselves volatile, because of the myriad factors that characterise and distinguish the major currency sectors.

Trading in a currency is, thus, very similar to adopting a long or short hedge in the commodity markets. Where physical or cash positions are being hedged, the company or enterprise involved needs to be informed of the forward position in order to determine whether this will obviate its strategies. However, as already demonstrated, a straight straddle position is more difficult to create due to interest rate differentials.

International banks do, however, initiate straddles to protect themselves from client positions. These are known as *swaps* and require matching of a long position with a short position, or vice versa. This leaves the bank exposed only to the interest rate differential involved until the clients eventually consummate and close out their positions. This technique should be understood in the absence of a clearing house in the forward market.[5] Under these circumstances, the only guarantee that a bank has that the customer transacting business will settle the account is the credit rating it assigns to him. This is why foreign exchange clients are, for the most part, large corporations and others considered to be of the highest credit quality. Nevertheless, by executing an order for the client, the bank is still at risk should the customer renege or default. So the market maker reduces its own liability by swap transactions.

Forward transactions are normally completed by banks for one, three, six, nine and twelve months. In some cases, transactions may be completed for five years but trading of this nature is not normally the rule but the exception. Transactions in the shorter dates are much more common although not all currencies will have every month traded actively. Supply and demand will affect a currency's forward value and at times even convertible currencies will not trade in every month.

It can also be very difficult to plot out the various settlement months in yield curve fashion in order to determine future expectations concerning forward prices without an understanding of what are known, in market parlance, as *leads* and *lags*. These are factors which affect forward prices. For instance, if a bank had an outstanding position in Deutschmarks maturing in October and expected a revaluation of the mark in November, it might take action depending upon the nature of the position. If the position was long, the bank may wish to lag the anticipated revaluation in order to hold marks past the putative date. A short position may require an accelerated settlement, or lead.

Foreign exchange markets can be found in all the major money centres around the world and the price that they quote for a currency will normally only vary according to the time lag involved. Unlike other financial markets, the forex markets are almost continuous on an international scale and there are very few hours in a day when a transaction is not being completed.

ARTIFICIAL CURRENCIES

Even from this brief discussion it should be apparent that currency fluctuations can have serious consequences for businesses, international organisations, the major money markets and domestic interest rate structures. It is best highlighted by FAS 8 in accounting terms in the United States although any organisation, commercial or otherwise, can feel its effects. Since the late 1960s, several means of mitigating risk have developed in accounting for currency fluctuations by using what have become known as *artificial currencies*. These currency units attempt to ameliorate the effect of holding one prime currency by replacing it with a unit not subject to violent price fluctuations.

Currently, artificial currencies come in two varieties – *Special Drawing Rights* (SDRs), and other *basket currencies*. These two types have very different origins but are both becoming increasingly popular with both governmental and, to a lesser but growing extent, commercial bodies. Although the SDR is in itself a basket currency, a distinction must be drawn between it and other baskets because the SDR was originally proposed as a substitute for the dollar as a reserve asset and not simply as a means of spreading risk. However, the slow but increasing popularity of the SDR with governments and some commercial organisations has proven that it has wider appeal than originally thought.

The idea of an artificial currency which would play a central role in the new international payments system designed at Bretton Woods, was first conceived by John Maynard Keynes but it was not until the late 1960s that the IMF practically proposed the use of SDRs. As the dollar came under increasing pressure on the foreign exchanges, its role as the premier reserve asset also came into doubt. If the dollar fell on the exchanges, then each central bank that held it saw its assets dwindle in value. This became especially true after the demise of the Smithsonian agreement. Therefore, the SDR was put forward as an alternative reserve asset to add an element of stability to the international monetary system.

SDRs may be created by fiat of the IMF in accord with its charter. They are nothing more than book-keeping entries, substituting for dollars or other reserve currencies when the member country assents to the substitution. The SDR has undergone several metamorphoses, as has the international monetary system as a whole, which have changed its nature. Originally in 1969, the SDR was defined in terms of the quantity of gold equal to one United States dollar. After convertibility was suspended two years later, the SDR gained what the dollar had lost, 8 per cent, and became valued at $1.085. After the Smithsonian devaluation, it increased in value to $1.20. In 1974, it became valued on a basket basis, pegged against an aggregate, weighted average of sixteen currencies. As of January 1981, it was reduced to a slimmer basket representing the five major trading currencies.

According to the basket concept, an artificial currency is defined in terms of composition by the weighted group of currencies comprising it. Thus, if the US dollar is only 30 per cent of the weighted basket, a decline in the dollar would not damage the value of the basket that much. Furthermore, a decline in the dollar necessarily means that other hard currencies in the basket will probably gain in value, thereby protecting the nominal value of the artificial currency.

In interest rate terms, the rate set for the SDRs as a deposit offered by international banks is found by simply taking the eurodeposit rate for that currency and weighting it by the currency's composition in the basket. Depending upon international interest rate conditions, the aggregate interest rate could be higher or lower than rates offered on the United States dollar but the basket, nevertheless, provides an element of

TABLE 5.3   Composition of the Special Drawing Right

from January 1981	%	*prior*	%
US dollar	42	US dollar	33.0
Deutschmark	19	Deutschmark	12.5
sterling	13	sterling	7.5
French franc	13	French franc	7.5
Japanese yen	13	Japanese yen	7.5
		Italian lira	4.5
		Dutch guilder	5.5
		Canada dollar	4.5
		Belgian franc	4.0
		Saudi riyal	3.0
		Swedish krona	2.0
		Iranian riyal	1.5
		Australian dollar	1.5
		Spanish peseta	1.5
		Norwegian krone	1.5
		Austrian schilling	1.5
total	100		100*

* figure does not total due to rounding average weight.

SOURCE: IMF *Survey*

stability to the currency exposure during the holding period. The current composition of the SDR is shown in Table 5.3.

The other major artificial currency in use today is the European Unit of Account (EUA), a basket used by the European community members for accounting purposes. The EUA was preceded by the older European Currency Unit (ECU) but now is standard among the EEC member communities. The EUA is a basket of the nine currencies of the members of the EEC, weighted in terms of their size and standing within the Nine. Unlike the SDR, the EUA is not used as a commercial vehicle for accepting deposits by commercial banks although some eurobond issues have been denominated in it and its predecessor, the ECU.

Artificial currencies arose because of the intrinsic volatility in the international monetary system which made accounting for transnational and supranational bodies difficult. As long as the system remains in a state of flux because of floating exchange rates, they will continue to play an increasingly important role in international finance, providing an element of stability amidst the volatility of the current exchange rate regime.

NOTES

1. Not all of the country's reserves are necessarily available for investment. Most central banks have their own internal guidelines for determining how much cash must remain on hand to finance the country's average import bill or cover new issues of note and coin.
2. In the case of central banks, many mitigate risk of dollar volatility by holding part of their reserves in Special Drawing Rights with the International Monetary Fund.
3. For a thorough discussion of the types of exposure a corporation can experience see Andreas Prindl, *Foreign Exchange Risk* (New York and London: John Wiley, 1972).
4. Exchange rates quoted in countries which are not the home of either currency involved are known as cross-rates. A dealer in London quoting a dollar/Swiss franc rate is said to be quoting a cross-rate.
5. Foreign currencies are now also traded on the Chicago commodity markets and as such are part of the futures market rather than the forward market.

SUGGESTED READING

Raymond Connix, *Foreign Exchange Today* (Cambridge: Woodhead Faulkner, 1978).

Paul Einzig, *A Textbook of Foreign Exchange* (London: Macmillan, 1973).

Paul Einzig, *Leads and Lags* (London: Macmillan, 1968).

H. Robert Heller, *International Monetary Economics* (Englewood Cliffs, N.J.: Prentice-Hall, 1972).

Andreas Prindl, *Foreign Exchange Risk* (New York and London: John Wiley, 1972).

Heinz Riehl and R. Rodriguez, *Foreign Exchange Markets* (New York: McGraw-Hill, 1977).

Robert Solomon, *The International Monetary System, 1946–76: An Insider's View* (New York: Harper and Row, 1978).

Rudi Weisweiller, *Foreign Exchange* (London: Allen and Unwin, 1972).

6 Options Markets

For many years futures markets in shares have existed in the major equity markets around the world. They were organised along over-the-counter lines in that they had no one central trading location within their respective financial centres. Beginning in 1973, this concept was formalised into an organised futures market for American share options when the Chicago Board Options Exchange (CBOE) was instituted. Most appropriately, the new futures market *per se* was located in the capital of commodity futures in the United States. Since that time, several other options exchanges have also been founded; four in the US, two in Europe, and one in Canada.

The futures markets in shares operate in much the same fashion as the commodity futures markets. Basically, they enable an investor to purchase an option giving him the right to buy or sell a specified number of shares at a future date, at a specific price. For this right, the investor either pays or receives money but one other important aspect from the commodity markets carries over here; the money involved is only a fraction of the market value of the shares concerned. Thus, a great deal of leverage also exists with options. However, despite these similarities, there are fundamental differences between the options and commodity markets due to the nature of the underlying instruments upon which they are based.[1]

Options have enjoyed phenomenal success since they were introduced formally in the United States. But as with all relatively new financial instruments, they have also come under severe criticism and poor publicity. They have been decried as highly leveraged, mini equity markets suitable only for speculators and been praised as having valuable hedging potential for the conservative investor. Before any attempt can be made here to examine these arguments or examine the economics of options trading, a full explication of their nature is necessary. Unlike the financial instruments we have examined thus far,

121

options have no clear economic importance since they neither raise money for a company nor present their holder with any tangible economic asset.

CHARACTERISTICS OF OPTIONS

Jean-Jacques Rousseau once warned his readers in advance of some very difficult concepts in his *Social Contract* by asking them to bear with him until the end of the discourse. The same caveat should be issued here; options terminology is extremely difficult at first glance and should be approached slowly.

By the term option is meant the right to buy or sell shares in the future at a specific price. The future date is a set date in a series of months assigned to certain options. For instance, an option in a certain share may expire in February, May, August and November or in January, April, July and October. After the terminal date, the option is worthless. The price at which it is struck is appropriately called the *striking price*.

Two types of options exist – *calls* and *puts*. Although their names are somewhat inelegant they do adequately reflect the nature of the options themselves. A call option is an option to buy. In turn, it may either be bought or sold. For example, one who buys a call buys the right to buy shares until a certain month at a specific price. Conversely, one who sells a call sells the right to buy his shares to someone else under otherwise similar circumstances.

Call options, as commodity contracts, are neither functional nor disfunctional until one actually utilises them. Buyers and sellers of calls have very different investment objectives and from even a brief description it will be seen how the detractors and adherents of options trading line up opposite each other.

Call buyers speculate on the future price rise of the underlying equity involved. For instance, assume that the current price of XYZ is $27 per share. An investor assumes that its price will rise in the near future and would like to participate in the profits involved. However, he does not want to pay $2700 for 100 shares. But he can purchase options at $30/share. For the options, he will pay $1\frac{1}{4}$, or $125 for 100 shares (all United States options represent 100 underlying shares).

This option price will vary, depending upon the month of expiration chosen. For instance, assume that this purchase was made in November and the investor chose an XYZ April 30 (expires in April, striking price of $30/share). His other choices and their striking and market prices are

TABLE 6.1   Options striking prices

option and strike	Jan	Apr	July	stock close
XYZ25	$2\frac{1}{8}$	$2\frac{1}{2}$	$2\frac{3}{4}$	27
XYZ p25*	$\frac{3}{8}$	$\frac{3}{4}$	1	27
XYZ 30	$\frac{3}{4}$	$1\frac{1}{4}$	$1\frac{1}{2}$	27
XYZ 35	$\frac{1}{8}$	$\frac{1}{4}$	$\frac{3}{8}$	27

* put, all others calls

shown in Table 6.1. As can be seen, the longer the life of the option the higher its market price. This illustrates the basic economic aspect of an option: the longer the life of the option the more value it possesses as a short-lived economic asset.

If the investor was correct and the price of XYZ rises to $35 per share, the option will also appreciate. The extent will again depend upon the life of the option but obviously it will be worth at least $500 (100 × $5). The investor then has two choices – he can sell the option at $500, realising a profit of $375, or he can exercise his full options rights and buy the shares at $30 each. Then he may immediately sell them at $35. Admittedly, this second avenue is somewhat supererogatory since the first road to profit is much simpler.

Had the shares moved in the opposite direction and stayed below $30 until the option expired the investor would have lost only the amount he had originally committed. This illustrates another difference between options and commodity markets: options losses are limited to the original investment while commodity contracts can theoretically decline the entire face value of the contracts themselves.

Essentially, the call buyer is a speculator who, for a fraction of the share price, can participate in the full gain if the shares do appreciate. On the opposite side of the coin, however, is the call seller who utilises options for quite a different purpose.

Call sellers, or *writers* as they are more commonly known, sell options against shares they already own in order to enhance the shares' performance. Using the same prices for XYZ cited above, assume that an investor purchases 100 shares at $27. The shares pay a dividend of $1 per year. If he holds them for 6 months he will receive $50 in dividends. However, in order to augment the return he may sell the same option at $125 with a striking price of $30. His six month return is now $175 with only one stipulation; if the shares rise above $30 he is liable to exercise at that price. Thus, his total return for the six months would be $475.

Call writing also provides an element of downside protection in the event the shares depreciate in value. In our example, the $125 received for the sale also protects the investor against a $125 loss. By augmenting the shares' dividend yield, the options give a measure of added stability to the shares in the event of a price fall. It is this measure which is used by conservative minded investors who sell calls against positions in order to protect themselves.

Investors who sell calls against shares do, however, limit their chance of gain should the stock move above the striking price. If XYZ moved over $30 per share in the example above, the option seller would normally have his shares called away unless he purchased them back at a price higher than that at which he originally sold them.

This brief example illustrates the two sided nature of call options. The other type of option – the put – also has a dualistic nature but is somewhat more difficult to understand since it is an option to sell.

A put is so named because it suggests that the seller of a put (that is, a seller of an option to sell) may have the stock put to him by the buyer at the striking price if the shares fall in value. For example, an investor eyes XYZ at 27 and decides, as did our call buyer, that it is undervalued. He then discovers that if he sells a put at 25 he will receive $\frac{3}{4}$ of a point ($75). If the shares should rise to 30 at expiration date, there is no chance that any put holder will exercise the option and sell shares to him at 25; doing so would involve an immediate loss for the put holder. So, in this case the put writer has guessed correctly and made money in the process.

However, if the shares had fallen to 20, the writer could feel certain to be exercised at 25 and have stock 'put' to him. This amply illustrates the risk intrinsic to the put selling process. Naturally, in all of the cases outlined here, positions can be closed out prior to expiration in order to avoid an exercise notice.

It can be seen that both call buying and put selling have a common trait – they are the more speculative of the activities associated with each type of option. Put buying, as call selling, is the conservative side of this particular option coin.

One who purchases a put buys the right to sell stock to another at a particular striking price. This will normally only occur when a stock falls below its striking price. Then the holder may exercise his option or close out the position at a profit. Oddly enough, the price of put options moves inversely with the price of the underlying shares. When examining calls we noted that the price of the option moves up with the price of the stock; thus, an option with a striking price of 30 whose underlying shares stand at 35 must have a nominal value of at least 5.

Puts move in the opposite direction. If the put had a striking price of 30 and the shares stood at 25, the option would have a nominal value of 5. This inverse relationship is perhaps the most difficult point to grasp when confronting puts – put prices rise as the shares depreciate.

Who uses put buying as an investment strategy? Mainly, put purchases are another form of short selling. If an investor thought XYZ was overvalued at 27, he might buy a put at 25. When the shares move down his position will gain and he has effectively shorted the stock by using only a fraction of their market value.

Although this strategy appears as speculative as call buying, it can be used to protect share positions. The investor who purchases shares at 27 and buys a put at 25 insures himself against loss during the life of the option since the put's appreciation will match the stock's potential depreciation. It is this mirror image nature of a put versus a call which makes it an ideal defensive instrument. Utilised on its own, put buying is tantamount to short selling; when used against existing share positions it affords excellent hedging protection.

PRICES AND PREMIUMS

As already seen, options prices vary depending upon their life spans. Those with a long life will fetch a higher price than those with short lives. Thus, the actual market value of the underlying shares plus market expectations for the future value of the shares are the two variables affecting the market price of options themselves. Both factors in turn are affected by a time–risk factor; that is, future developments which may affect either or both markets. The longer any financial instrument is so exposed, the higher its price premium must be.

Table 6.1 illustrated that a share with a market price of $27 may have options with different striking prices attached. Assume for a moment that striking prices exist at $40, $45 and $50.[2] The current value of the underlying shares is $47. This can be seen in Table 6.2 where artificial prices and premiums have been assigned to each month and striking price.

Those options at a striking price of $40 in the nearest month must be valued at $7 and the $45 strike at $2; otherwise arbitrage would quickly take place bringing the anomalous prices into line. For instance, if the $40 option was valued at only $6\frac{1}{2}$, an arbitrageur could purchase the option for $650, immediately exercise it and simultaneously sell the shares at $47. His profit would be $50, before transaction costs.

TABLE 6.2   Options premiums

option and strike	Jan	Apr	July	stock close
XYZ 40	7	8	9	47
XYZ 45	2	3	4	47
XYZ 50	$\frac{1}{2}$	1	$1\frac{1}{2}$	47

When the option is worth only its nominal value, no premium exists.[3] However, if the $40 April option were priced at $9 rather than $8 the premium would be $1. As can be seen in Table 6.2, premiums are normally attached to longer lived options. This will, of course, be true in the case of those shares where investor expectations are high. In the event expectations are low, little if any premium will be found on in-the-money options.

But what of out-of-the-money options (where the striking price of the calls is above the market price of the underlying shares)? What determines the price of the $50 option in our example? In these cases, investor expectations play the only role. If the shares are expected to appreciate then that option will reflect it in price. Otherwise, it will sell for only a fraction of a point.

Options prices may at times behave somewhat independently; movements may be greater or less than the proportionate price movement in the shares. Thus, it would be incorrect to assume that options perfectly reflect share movements since investor expectations for stock can spill over into the options markets to the extent that buying fervour may reflect in options rather than equities. Cases such as these do give credence to the argument that options markets lure investors away from stock markets. When heavy volume in an option creates volatile prices it would appear that speculators seek the leverage afforded by options (in this case, calls) rather than turn to the share market.

Prices are not normally adversely affected, at least directly, by interest rates moving higher since options may not be purchased on margin. Rather, they must be paid for in full at time of purchase. Conversely, options provide a speculative market for those who normally buy shares on margin but do not want to pay high interest rates on their share debit amounts. However, insofar as high interest rates normally depress share prices, options prices will generally reflect their respective shares unless other economic factors help the shares run counter to the market.

OPTIONS STRATEGIES

In the previous sections we have discussed options in their simplest and singular sense; by using examples employing one type of option only or one used in a specific option/share strategy. There are, however, many more strategies employed, utilising a combination of puts and calls both together and on their own.

Although the intricacies of many of these strategies are beyond the scope of this discussion, their uses should be noted since they can have an impact upon options prices. Basically, strategies can be broken into two groups – those combining the same type of option and those mingling puts and calls.[4]

Within the first category, the major type of strategy is called *spreading*. Normally, a spread involves buying a call at one striking price and selling one at another price. This is sometimes referred to as an arbitrage operation but this is not an accurate description of the activity. Spreads may be bullish or bearish; that is, they may take different views as to the future of the stock involved.

A *bull spread* is employed when the investor feels the shares will appreciate. For instance, he may buy a November 30 option on a share and sell a November 40. This is shown in Table 6.3. What has been accomplished is this: if the shares appreciate to perhaps $42, the spread will be worth more and the positions may be closed out. Assume that, following the table, the 30 option was bought for $300 and the 40 sold for $50. The net cost for the transaction was thus $250.

If the shares appreciate to $42, the 30 option will have a nominal value of at least $12 and the 40 will be worth $2. When closing out of the position, the 30 will be sold netting a profit of $900 while the 40 will be bought back for $200. The entire transaction netted $750 for a $250 original spread.

TABLE 6.3   Bull spread

	Nov	stock close
open position		
XYZ 30	3	32
XYZ 40	$\frac{1}{2}$	32
close position		
XYZ 30	12	42
XYZ 40	2	42

The major virtue of spreading is that after the investor chooses his spread he knows immediately how much he stands to lose if the share price falls; in this case $250. He also knows exactly how much he will earn (at least minimally). In the example employed above the $750 earned is a payout of 3 to 1 for the risk capital originally employed. In other words, the reward outweighed the risk by 3 to 1.

Spreading may also be bearish with the investor selling the 30 series and buying the 40. Spreads also may be accomplished by combining options of different expiration dates (*time spreads*) or by combining three or more exercise prices in a multiple array (*butterfly spreads*).

Strategies involving a combination of puts and calls come in a variety of somewhat bewildering names. A *strip* combines two puts and a call of the same striking price and expiration while a *strap* combines two calls and a put with otherwise similar features. A *straddle* is a double option consisting of a put and a call with the same striking price.

For present purposes, it is most important to remember that options strategies may affect the price of options themselves and therefore a simple glance at prices in a newspaper may not tell the entire story regarding trading. For instance, assume that an investor was bearish on a stock and employed ten strips to support his position. By buying two puts at 30 and buying one call at 30 he is essentially taking out some cheap insurance in the event that his assumption proves incorrect. If the shares do not decline but rather appreciate, his call will help offset the loss of the put purchase. However, this will be reported in the options column in the press as ten call options at 30. If the shares are also at 30 this could be construed as an indication that investor expectations support the shares but an equal glance at the put activity would not support this. Therefore, the options columns must be read closely before any generalisations can be made about investor expectations.

THE DIMINISHING ASSET CONCEPT

At this stage, it should be apparent that options, whether puts or calls, have a very limited value as economic assets. But it would be incorrect to assume they have no economic value at all since their prices may fluctuate widely during their relatively short life spans. However, in most instances, options cannot be hypothecated as can shares or bonds because, as commodity contracts, they will soon be worthless unless exercised, regardless of present value.

For this reason, options are considered diminishing assets. This can

TABLE 6.4   Diminishing option value

	Jan	*stock close*
on November 1 XYZ 30	$\frac{3}{4}$	27
on January 20 XYZ 30	$\frac{1}{16}$	27

best be illustrated by holding the current market value of the underlying shares constant over the duration of the option's life. In Table 6.4, an out-of-the-money option is shown under such circumstances. If the value of the shares never rises above their current value, the option will become less valuable as expiry date approaches. Thus, the asset originally worth $75 will be virtually worthless on the last day of the option's life.

This phenomenon can also be seen in the original tax treatment of options employed in the United Kingdom. If an investor purchased a six month option for 100p and subsequently sold it in three months for 60p he was actually subject to a capital gain rather than the loss that has obviously incurred. According to the concept, as employed by the Inland Revenue Service, the real value of such an option should be 50p. (100 p at (6 months − 3 months) = 50p). By selling the option at 60p the investor has actually gained 10p over the diminishing time value of the option and must pay tax on it.

Tax treatment of options losses in the United States is less strict and follows the more traditional line of treating ostensible losses as losses. Therefore, the investor in this situation may claim the equivalent of a 40p loss on his position.

THE MARKETS

The United States

Options trading in America closely follows the patterns of share trading on the stock exchanges. Most of the listed options are those of shares traded on the New York Stock Exchange and, to a lesser extent, on the American Stock Exchange. As with share trading, a certain amount of overlap, or dual listing exists; especially between the CBOE and Amex as well as between the major and regional exchanges.

The largest options exchange in the United States and the world is the CBOE. Currently, it trades several hundred listed options, almost all of which trade on the NYSE in share form. When the CBOE originally began operations, all of its options business was conducted in calls only; puts were introduced in 1977 and have been assigned only in limited numbers. This is not surprising given the educative process needed surrounding options in general and puts in particular.

The other American options exchanges exist at the American, Philadelphia, Midwest and Pacific stock exchanges although the CBOE remains as the only exchange devoted solely to options. Criteria for listing share options differ among the exchanges, with the largest and most widely known companies being dealt on the CBOE and Amex. However, regardless of the capitalisation of the company involved, all listed share options are those of well-known companies whose shares are easily recognised and widely traded. This ensures (to an extent) that the parallel options trading will be relatively orderly.

One question arises when one approaches a study of options, especially for the first time. This centres around what is called *open interest* on the contracts themselves. Open interest is the number of contracts outstanding on each series of options. This interest, representing investor activity rather than a rate of money charged, is not controlled by an issuing or authorising body. Essentially, an option position may be created by either a buyer or seller and becomes complete when a party is found to complete the opposite side of the transaction.

An example helps make this process clearer. An options writer desires to sell calls and, after checking the available options and prices, contacts a broker and places an order. However, by doing so he is not selling an option which has been previously issued; when his transaction is confirmed he will in fact have created a new option (in volume terms). Thus, if he sold one call he has added one additional outstanding contract to the open interest position. If the position is subsequently closed a month later, the open interest will be reduced by one.

Options contracts are created by the desire of the investor rather than by an issuing body, as in the case of shares. In Table 6.5 the outstanding amount of shares of several leading US companies is shown along with the total amount of options outstanding against them. It can be seen that if all of these positions were to be exercised the price of the shares themselves could become quite volatile. The putative effects of this volume trading will be discussed in the next section here.

TABLE 6.5   Shares outstanding and options open interest
(September 1980)

company	shares outstanding (000)	open interest
General Motors	291 261	10 086 000
IBM	583 336	20 875 900
Polaroid	32 855	4 402 600
Exxon	437 188	3 908 900
Westinghouse	84 837	4 530 200

How options are traded can and does have a great deal to do with their volatility and price effect upon the underlying shares. As originally seen in Chapter 1, the type of trading system used on the floor of the exchange itself can at times have a serious impact upon trading patterns and prices. Whether or not the two major types of system in use have any intrinsic merits or faults is somewhat beyond the scope of this discussion but it should be noted that both perform equally well unless the market should come under severe strain.

The CBOE employs a *market maker* system while the Amex uses a *specialist* system supported by individual associate members who trade for their own account. The market maker system is one in which specified individuals 'make a market' in certain designated options on the exchange floor but who do not trade for their own account. The specialist system, on the other hand, incorporates a market maker function with a personal function; specialists may also trade for their own account. In either case these individuals provide liquidity on the exchange floors and are prohibited from refusing a trade unless it is unrealistically priced away from the current market.[5]

Among both market professionals and private investors a good deal of arbitrage occurs within the options markets themselves and also between options and share markets. This arbitrage activity should be distinguished from the spreading strategies mentioned previously. Basically, option arbitrage may be divided into two categories – dividend arbitrage and exercise arbitrage. Both involve dealings with the share markets.

Dividend arbitrage occurs when the option price for a call is cheaper in value than the stated quarterly dividend due to be paid on a share. The arbitrageur then exercises the option in time to receive the dividend, pocketing the difference before immediately re-selling the shares.

Exercise arbitrage occurs during the final week of an option series.

The process is very rapid and can occur within the space of a few moments and incorporates some of the principles mentioned in previous sections. During the last days of an option, arbitrageurs seek out those in-the-money calls where investor expectations are low; that is, they find calls with only nominal value. As expiry day approaches, anomalies may appear in the option price and an in-the-money call may actually slip to less than nominal value. If this happens, the call will be purchased and exercised and the shares immediately resold; the profit amounts to the difference between nominal value and the momentary slip.

The American options exchanges, by virtue of their size and accessibility to the equity markets, are more sophisticated than their two main European rivals at present. The European exchanges have been less successful in the first several years of operation due to problems not encountered by the American exchanges.

European Exchanges – Amsterdam and London

The European Options Exchange (EOE) was established in Amsterdam in 1978. At the time of writing, it trades some twenty-four options, representing shares from not one but six different national exchanges.[6] The internationalism of such an approach has led to problems hindering the EOE's further development. In order to be a truly international market, the EOE needs the consent of not only the respective monetary and exchange authorities in each country of the share involved but also of the national tax authorities. In many cases, either lack of acceptance or dilatory procedures have hindered the full development of the exchange.

The EOE does not suffer from one handicap that United States options exchanges do; it does not depend upon price movements in a single share market. This internationalism will perhaps, ultimately, be the key to success in many financial markets as a growing sense of cross border investment begins to affect what previously were purely domestic markets.

The operations of the EOE follow closely those of the CBOE, upon which it was based. The actual mechanics of exercise price, striking price and expiry months are identical and each option represents 100 shares of the underlying stock, with the exception of British stocks where a call represents 1000 shares. The market maker system is also used in conjunction with floor brokers who carry out orders on behalf of the general public. Equally, a clearing operation was established to facilitate the day-to-day operations of the exchanges.

The London Traded Options Market also opened in 1978, several months after the EOE commenced trading. The London exchange is still quite small, trading only a handful of British options after several years of existence. One major problem that the traded options market faces is that an over-the-counter market in options is still conducted in London, providing continuing competition to the organised market.

The Traded Options Market is situated on the floor of the London Stock Exchange and is backed by a clearing corporation. It uses a market maker system (all British stock jobbers may act as market makers) assisted by floor brokers. In this respect it is quite similar to the trading practices on the floor of both the EOE and Amex. Also, the mechanics of the American exchanges have been transplanted to London as well as to Amsterdam; striking prices, expiry months and other options terminology closely adhere to the original CBOE model.

The French Option Model

As we have seen, the organised options exchanges all proceed along the American model. However, there are other options markets around the world, normally operating within the domestic stock exchanges and following local financial tradition. The French options market is one example which illustrates how options can be used in other methods from the ones already described.

In Chapter 1, the basic mechanics of the French Bourse were noted. As noted, two types of settlement market exist for shares – the *marché au comptant* (cash market) and the *marché au terms* (forward market). If one purchases shares in the former, he settles the transaction immediately; if he settles in the latter he is obliged to pay in one month. If he opts for a conditional trade, he may cancel out his purchase prior to settlement date but will pay a premium (*prime*) to do so. Thus, a seller in the conditional forward market, if he receives the *prime*, is analagous to an options writer who sees his option expire unexercised.

In addition to this option-type share dealing, a separate options market exists on the Paris Bourse. Puts (*options de vente*) and calls (*options d'achat*) are traded and extend up to nine months into the future. The basic mechanics are also similar to American options. But given the nature of share dealing in a cash and forward market environment, options in France occupy less of a central position in investment strategy than they do in other markets because the *prime* in the forward market must actually be considered a type of option.

OPTIONS PROBLEMS

We have already seen that options present two immediate and perceptible problems – one educative and the other a matter of definition. In short, options can be difficult to understand both from the public's point of view as well as the taxman's. However, two other problems surround options trading which are even more fundamental in nature.

The first of these returns to a discussion that has been reiterated throughout this survey in different forms; namely, do options (as speculative instruments) siphon off funds which otherwise might have found their way into the equity markets? This question must necessarily be posed at the American markets since the European exchanges are still too young to answer this question.

It is unlikely that options trading (that is, speculative positions, including spreading) will appeal to a share investor whose interest lies in capital growth and/or dividend accumulation. Thus, when posing this question one must level it at that investor who is most likely to utilise options rather than shares if the leverage factor is in his favour. This naturally leads to that investor who buys shares in over-the-counter securities (normally the most speculative and cheapest in dollar terms of US shares).

In a study published in 1977, the Management Analysis Center concluded for the CBOE that options do not provide competition for risk capital which might otherwise find its way into primary or secondary distributions of shares for fledging companies.[7] This study is somewhat analagous to the study done by the NYSE to determine the effect of increasing amounts of debt capital on the new issues equity market, mentioned in earlier chapters. The options study focuses around one central fact mentioned earlier here: most options transactions take the form of writing strategies against existing share positions. Options writers are not speculators of the sort that would necessarily commit risk capital to the new issues market for new or small companies.

However, there are other problems raised by options which do pose problems, suggested by the same type of common sense logic that answered the previous question. For instance, the leverage factor options offer is acknowledged as a substitute for margin trading in US shares. An investor faced with the possibility of purchasing 100 shares of a $50 stock on margin might incur a sizeable cost for nine months funding his debit account. If he can purchase an option satisfying his expectations for the same amount he can achieve the same result without depositing $2500 (at a 50% margin requirement). This leaves the $2500 free for investment in other areas as well.

While this leverage factor does not affect over-the-counter United States companies, too small to qualify for either margin trading or options listing, the leverage analogy still bears some validity. Since otc shares cannot be protected by automatic stop–loss orders (used on Exchanges) the amount of capital invested is subject to greater risk than it might be if invested in a listed equity. Therefore, if the amount of investment is considered totally at risk then these stocks share a trait with options.

The second problem confronting options concerns their price volatility and manner in which they are traded; a trait obviously also shared with equities. In order to best illustrate this point one must be forced into a *reductio ad absurdam* of sorts.

The options exchanges protect investors and options positions by limiting the amount of contracts that any one investor may hold in any one contract month. However, as said earlier, the amount of open interest on options is not controlled. Therefore, it is possible that more options may be outstanding than there are shares to cover the positions. If this occurred, serious problems could develop in actual share prices. But more importantly, it is doubtful if either the market maker or specialist system could actually handle such a situation. Although it would be unreasonable to expect either system to absorb an infinite number of contract positions this does point out that a heavy volume in any month position (heavier than anticipated or historically experienced) could have a wide-ranging effect in more than one market sector.

It should be noted that the long term uses and economic effects of the options markets will obviously take substantial time to become clear since the instruments and their peculiarities and characteristics are still somewhat novel. However, a more widespread use of covered writing and put buying (hedging) strategies could substantially alter the nature of equity investment risk if these techniques prove compatible with prevalent investor psychology.

NOTES

1. The term option can also be used in the European commodity markets. In certain commodities, gold being one example, options are issued on the commodity contracts. Thus, a commodity option is an option on a commodity contract and its price moves in conjunction with the contract on the underlying commodity.
2. The striking price of an option series will depend upon the price movement of the underlying shares. A stock moving from $20 to $40 within a nine month period might well have options strike prices at 20, 25, 30, 35, 40. If the shares remain at $40, the lower priced options will eventually expire and not be replaced, reflecting the shares' new price level.
3. In options parlance, the term 'premium' is usually used to denote what is known as the total option price. This chapter will, however, refer to the term 'premium' as a true premium; that is, the additional value attached to an in-the-money call above its nominal value.
4. For a thorough explanation of various option strategies one may consult Max Ansbacher, *The New Options Market*, (New York: Walker, 1975). Call option strategies are discussed within a portfolio context by R. C. Merton, M. S. Scholes and M. Gladstein in 'The Returns and Risk of Alternative Call Option Portfolio Investment Strategies', *Journal of Business*, April 1978, pp. 183–242.
5. This does not include limit orders but only unrealistic market orders.
6. Several American shares also have outstanding options on the EOE as well as on the United States exchanges.
7. S. M. Robbins, R. B. Stobaugh, F. L. Sterling, and T. H. Howe, *The Impact of Exchange-Traded Options on the Market for New Issues of Common Stock of Small Companies* (Cambridge, Mass.: Management Analysis Center, 1977).

SUGGESTED READING

Max Ansbacher, *The New Options Market* (New York: Walker, 1975).
Henry Clasing, *The Dow Jones Irwin Guide to Put and Call Options* (Homewood: Dow Jones Irwin, 1978).

R. C. Merton, M. S. Scholes and M. Gladstein, 'The Returns and Risk of Alternative Call Option Portfolio Investment Strategies', *Journal of Business*, April 1978.

S. M. Robbins, R. B. Stobaugh, F. L. Sterling and T. H. Howe, *The Impact of Exchange-Traded Options on the Market for New Issues of Common Stock of Small Companies* (Cambridge, Mass.: Management Analysis Center, 1977).